JAHB: The Hazy Beginning

Mike Spiritfair Marty

Get a JAHB, LLC: Milwaukee

Bibliographic Data

©2006 Michael Spiritfair Marty (Chapters 1-3)
       (Completion date: April 21, 2006)

All rights reserved. No part of this artistic expression may be used or reproduced in any manner whatsoever without prior written permission of the author, except in the case of brief quotations embodied in reviews.

Get a JAHB, LLC (Publisher)
Mike Spiritfair Marty (Imprint) is the author and arranger of this
       particular expression of the Word of God (for antitrust
       competitive purposes)

Cover art designer (2026):
Interior art illustrator (2026):

Library of Congress Cataloging-in-Publication Data
Names: Marty, Mike Spiritfair, author.
Title: Just another holy book / Mike Spiritfair Marty, BLS, BA, MBA.
Description: Get a JAHB paperback First Edition. | Milwaukee, WI : Get a JAHB, LLC, 2026.
Identifiers: LCCN 2025922293 | ISBN 9798998577321 (paperback)
Subjects: LCSH: Christianity--History--By period. The Bible--Modern texts and versions. Political science--Political theory--Consensus--Consent of the governed. Law--Religious law in general--Comparative religious law. Language and literature--Literature--Collections--Literary extracts. BISAC: BIBLES / Multiple Translations / Text | LAW / General | POLITICAL SCIENCE / Religion, Politics & State | RELIGION / Christian Theology / History
Classification: LCC BS125-198.B52 M32 2025 V1 | DDC 209.019 M32 V1

First Edition: Has general table of contents but no index

Dedication

Dedicated to Hus and Wycliffe (and Lynnae)

Introduction

This holy remix of the Christian Bible is about one-eighth the length, and it employs excerpts from nine orthodox versions: King James (KJV), New American (NAB), New American Standard (NASB), New International (NIV), New King James (NKJV), Revised Standard (RSV), The Amplified (TAB), Today's English (TEV), and The Living (TLB).

A "+" has been placed in front of all verses in which one or more words have been changed from the original verse. A "+" has not been placed in front of verses in which only punctuation or capitalization has been altered nor in front of verses in which, for example, "Job" has been respelled as "Joebh," or in which YAH-way, God, Christ, He, or the LORD have been interchanged with each other. Sometimes, though, especially perhaps in the first two sections (History and Poetry), words have been mixed all around and their order changed, though the verse listing is intended to show in what way the words have been rearranged. If there are a lot of verse references for a short verse, presumably the word order has been significantly adjusted to create a particular idea.

Also, Tab 1 is for the setting, Tab 2 is for "God speaks," Tab 3 is for a human speaker, Tab 4 is for the adversarial spirit, and Tab 5 is for a human critic--generally, this is the structure.

This rearranged version is intended not to replace the Bible but to excite people to read their unabridged versions, though, ideally, *Just Another Holy Book* is an improvement in some aspects over the unabridged versions. A condensed work, however, is rarely, if ever, able to match the value of a great original.

Table of Contents

Bibliographic Data 2
Dedication 3
Introduction 4
The Hazy Beginning 8
  History (H) 9
    One--Noah 9
    Two--Zechariah 16
    Three--Jehoshaphat 20
    Four--Jonah 23
    Five--Mattathias 27
    Six--David 30
    Seven--Daniel 35
    Eight--Solomon 38
  Poetry (Po) 42
    One 42
    Two--Susanna 44
    Three--Joebh 48
    Four--Ruth 53
    Five--Abishag 57
    Six--Sarah 60
    Seven--Esther 64
    Eight--Kelli 68
    Nine--Onias 75
  Piety (Pi) 80
    One--Simon 80
    Two 90
    Three--Ezra 100
    Four--Elijah 111

Five--Baruch 119
Six.. 126
Works Cited 133
History 133
Poetry 135
Piety 137

Just Another Holy Book (JAHB)

JAHB: The Hazy Beginning

-- 2 Esdras 14:47 (TEV)[1]

---
[1] *Holy*

The Hazy Beginning

-- *Nicomachean Ethics*, Aristotle

-- Numbers 16:22
(New King James Version)[2]

---
[2] *Spirits*

History (H)

One--Noah

1. I will now try to summarize in a single book that which is noted in the scripture of truth.

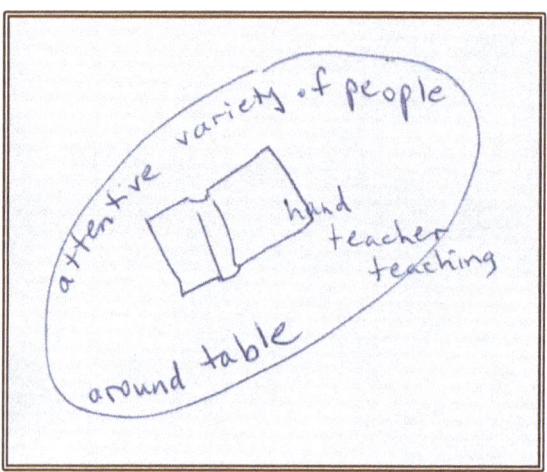

2. The bulk of material can be overwhelming, but I have attempted to simplify it for all readers. Writing such a summary is a difficult task, demanding hard work and sleepless nights. It is as difficult as preparing a banquet that people of different tastes will enjoy. But I am happy to undergo this hardship in order to please my readers.

+3. I will leave the responsibility for exact details to the original authors, and attempt to give only a summary outline.

4. I am not the builder of a new house who is concerned with every detail of the structure, but simply a painter whose only concern is to make the house look attractive. So then, without any further comment, I will begin my story.

5. A heavy burden lies on all of us from the day of our birth until the day we go back to the earth, the mother of us all.

We are confused and fearful,³ dreading the day of our death--all of us from the king on his splendid throne wearing royal robes and a crown, to the humblest person dressed in burlap and living in poverty.

+6. Long ago, each different group of people began to make idols in the various cities in which they lived.

7. The people of Babylon made idols of the god Succoth Benoth; the people of Cuth, idols of Nergal; the people of Hamath, idols of Ashima; the people of Ivvah, idols of Nibhaz and Tartak; and the people of Sepharvaim sacrificed their children as burnt offerings to their gods Adrammelech and Anammelech.

8. In early times the famous giants were born, a mighty race skilled in war. They perished for lack of prudence, perished through their folly.

9. Later generations have dwelt in the land, but the way to understanding they have not known. They did not find the path to Wisdom or ever reach her. Their children also failed. She has not been heard of in Canaan, nor seen in Teman. The sons of Hagar who seek knowledge on earth, the⁴ merchants of Midian, the phrasemakers seeking knowledge, these have not known the way to Wisdom, nor have they her paths in mind.

+10. In these days there were no wages for man or beast; and for him who went out or came in there was no safety because of his enemies.

11. And every man cried out to his god.

+12. But YAH-way is greater than any other god.

13. Noah was a pleasure to YAH-way. He was a righteous man, blameless among the people of his time, for he walked with God. And Noah did according to all that the YAH-way

---

³*Confused*
⁴*Idols*

commanded him.

14. "Man greatly beloved, understand the words that I speak to you, and stand upright, for I am God and not man, the Holy One in the midst of you."

15. "Obey me and be perfect--blameless, whole-hearted, complete."[5]

16. "I will instruct thee and teach thee in the way which thou shalt go: I will guide thee with mine eye."

17. "Behold, all those who are angered at you will be shamed and dishonored; those who contend with you will be as nothing, and will perish."

18. "Do not be afraid. I am your shield."

19. "Be quiet and listen to me, and I will teach you how to be wise."

20. "O God, the God of the spirits of all flesh, lead me and guide me."

21. "For the Spirit of God has made me, in whose hand is the life of every living thing, and the breath of all mankind."

22. "And He is high above all the peoples."

+23. "The earth is satisfied with the fruit of His works. He causes the grass to grow for the cattle, and vegetation from the labor of man, so that food may be brought forth from the earth."[6]

24. "Ask the animals, and they will teach you, or the birds of the air, and they will tell you; or speak to the earth, and it will teach you, or let the fish of the sea inform you.

---

[5]*YAH-way*
[6]*Instruct*

Which of all these does not know that the hand of YAH-way has done this?"

+25. And Noah began to be a mighty one on the earth, one desired by women.

26. So Noah went forth, and his sons and his wife and his sons' wives with him.

27. Then God spoke to Noah, saying: "Behold, I establish My covenant with you and with your descendants after you."

+28. Then this truth was given me in secret, as though whispered in my ear.

29. It came in a nighttime vision as others slept. I sat astonished. Fear gripped me; I trembled and shook with terror. The hair of my flesh stood up.

30. "You shall not go after other gods, the gods of the peoples who are all[7] around you."

31. "For all the gods of the nations are [lifeless] idols."

32. "If you have understanding, hear this."

33. "In years to come, tell your children about it."

34. "Consider the work of God."

35. "Who gives intuition? Or who has given understanding to the heart?"

+36. "It is the spirit in a man, the breath of YAH-way, that gives him understanding."

37. "You must never worship another god."

38. "These are the words that you shall speak to the sons of

---

[7] *Whispered*

Israel."

39. "Watch yourselves carefully, since you did not see any form on the day[8] YAH-way spoke to you at Horeb from the midst of the fire, lest you act corruptly and make a graven image for yourselves in the form of any figure, the likeness of male or female, the likeness of any animal that is on the earth, the likeness of any winged bird that flies in the sky, the likeness of anything that creeps on the ground, the likeness of any fish that is in the water below the earth."

40. "And beware, lest you lift up your eyes to heaven and see the sun and the moon and the stars, and be drawn away and worship them and serve them."

+41. "YAH-way, the Holy One of Israel, is our shelter and strength, always ready to help in times of trouble."

42. "Him you shall fear, Him you shall worship, and to Him you shall offer sacrifice."

+43. "Behold, as the eyes of servants look to the hand of their masters, as the eyes of a maid to the hand of her mistress, so our eyes look to YAH-way our God, that He may teach us the good way in which we should walk."[9]

44. After this I awoke and looked around.

+45. So Noah fed his people according to the integrity of his heart, and guided them by the skillfulness of his hands.

46. Light and understanding and wisdom was found in him.

+47. One day a man came to Noah.

---

[8] *Intuition*
[9] *Beware*

+48. And Noah arose and came to the man and said to him, "Do you come peaceably?"

49. And he said, "Peaceably."

50. This man was born in Babylon. The Babylonians had an idol named Bel.

+51. The man kept asking about Noah and his family.

52. "Why don't you worship Bel? And have you no king?"[10]

+53. Noah answered, "I do not worship idols made with human hands. I worship only the living God, who is the Lord of all mankind. I worship YAH-way. He is the only living God. And as for a king, what would he do for us?"

+54. And the man said to Noah, "I will depart from you to my own land and to my kinsmen."

+55. But Noah said, "Please do not leave. If you stay with us, whatever good the YAH-way will do to us, the same we will do to you."

+56. But he turned, and went away.

+57. And as soon as the man was gone, Noah heard these words.

58. "Listen to Me, and take heed. I have put My words in your mouth and have covered you in the shadow of My hand, that I may fix the new heavens as a tabernacle, and lay the foundations of a new earth, and say to Zion, You are My people."[11]

+59. Many years later, after YAH-way had given the Israelites of Zion rest from all their enemies round about them, Apollonius from Greece arrived, pretending to be on a peace

---

[10] *Bel*
[11] *Zion*

mission.

60. He led his troops, who were fully armed, in a parade outside the city. Suddenly he commanded his men to kill everyone who had come out to see them. They rushed into the city and murdered a great many people.

+61. Noah was taken away.

62. He was oppressed and afflicted, though he had done no violence, nor was any deceit in his mouth.

+63. Every Jew who refused to adopt the Greek invader's way of life was threatened with death.

+64. His captors encouraged him to submit to the pressure. But Noah made a decision worthy of his gray hair and advanced age.

65. All his life he had lived in perfect obedience to God, so he replied, "Kill[12] me, here and now. For the present I might be able to escape what you could do to me, but whether I live or die, I cannot escape the YAH-way. Many young people would think that I had denied my faith after I was ninety years old. If I die bravely now, it will show that I deserved my long life."

66. "The end of a thing is better than its beginning."

67. "I go the way of all the earth."

68. Those with him were amazed at his courage and at his willingness to suffer.

+69. So Noah died.

+70. "But you, Israel, are My servant, the descendants of Noah My friend."

---

[12]*Threatened*

71.   "Fear not, for I am with you; be not dismayed, for I am your God. I will strengthen you, yes, I will help you."[13]

Two--Zechariah

1.   Then the Spirit of God clothed Zechariah.

+2.   YAH-way, the God of Israel, said to him, "Write down in a book everything that I tell you."

3.   "Now listen and give heed, O Israel."

4.   "This is what YAH-way has said."

5.   "Circumcise the foreskin of your [mind and] heart."

6.   "For the YAH-way is God of gods and the Lord of lords, the great God, mighty and awesome, who has no favorites and accepts no bribes."

7.   "He makes sure that orphans and widows are treated fairly, and shows His love for the alien by giving him food and clothing."

8.   "Love ye therefore the stranger, for you were once aliens yourselves in the land of Egypt."[14]

9.   "Have reverence for YAH-way your God. Be faithful; you shall serve God, and to God shalt thou cling closely."

+10.   "It is the YAH-way who forms the spirit of man within him."

---

[13] *Escape*
[14] *Circumcise*

11. "Every creature that is alive, all the animals of the earth, shall be yours to eat, in addition to the green vegetables and plants."

12. "Be strong and conduct yourselves like men."

+13. The next day Zechariah was settling disputes among the people, and he was kept busy from morning till night.

+14. When Zechariah's father-in-law saw how much time this was taking, he said, "Why are you trying to do all this alone, with people standing here all day long to get your help?"

+15. "Because the people come to me to ask for God's decisions," Zechariah told him. "I am their judge, deciding who is right and who is wrong, and instructing them in the YAH-way."[15]

16. "You are not acting wisely," his father-in-law replied.

17. "You and the people with you will wear yourselves out. This job is too heavy a burden for you to try to handle all by yourself."

18. "Now listen to my voice: I shall give you counsel."

19. "It is right for you to represent the people and bring their disputes to YAH-way."

20. "Explain to them how they should live."

21. "But in addition, you should also look among all the people for God-fearing men of truth, who hate unjust gain."

22. "And appoint them as leaders of the people."

23. "And let them judge the people at all times; and let

---

[15] *Strong*

it be that every major dispute they will bring to you, but every minor matter they themselves will judge. Thus, your burden will be lightened, since they[16] will bear it with you."

+24. Zechariah listened to his father-in-law and did everything he said.

+25. From year to year, Zechariah reigned over all Israel; and he administered justice and equity to all his people. He behaved wisely in all his ways, and the YAH-way was with him.

26.   "I will have compassion on the house of Judah; and I will save them--not by bow, sword or battle, or by horses and horsemen, but by YAH-way their God."

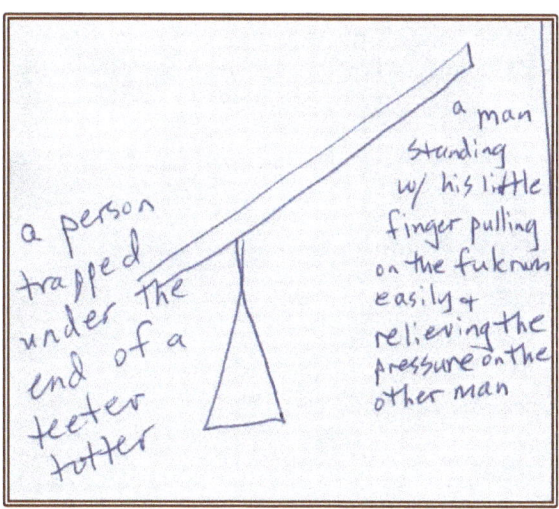

+27. When he was old, he called together all the people of Israel.

28.   "Hear, O Israel. Peace be with you, do not be afraid."

29.   "Soon I will be going the way of all the earth. My time has come."

---

[16] Judge

30. "Incline your heart to the YAH-way of Israel."[17]

31. "He is unique, and who can make Him change?"

+32. "A man who walks with integrity walks securely, but he who magnifies the gate of his house invites destruction."

+33. And all the people said, "Amen! O our God, we do not always know what to do, but our eyes are upon You."

+34. Then Zechariah distributed among all the people, among the whole multitude of Israel, both the women and the men, to everyone a loaf of bread, a piece of meat, and a cake of raisins. So all the people departed, everyone to his house.

+35. And Zechariah bowed his head and worshiped the YAH-way of his master Noah, who had led him into the way of truth.

36. So he died.

+37. (These names and events all come from very ancient records.)[18]

Three--Jehoshaphat

1. Then the fear of YAH-way fell upon Jehoshaphat. Jehoshaphat was frightened, and he hastened to consult the YAH-way.

2. He announced that all the people of Judah should go without food for a time, in penitence.

---
[17] *Equity*
[18] *Ancient*

3. He did right in YAH-way's sight, but not with a perfect or blameless heart.

4. He was the one who cried out to the God of Israel:

5. "Oh, that you would wonderfully bless me and enlarge my territory!"

6. "Please be with me in all that I do, and keep me from harm so that I will be free from pain."

+7. As long as he followed the paths of YAH-way, he prospered.

+8. Thus Jehoshaphat grew powerful because he lived resolutely in the[19] presence of the YAH-way, his God.

9. Then I heard the voice of someone speaking to me.

10. "Take all the fighting men with you and go to Ai, for it is now yours to conquer; see, I have given into your hand the king of Ai, and his people, his city, and his land."

11. He armed all his men, not so much by encouraging them to trust in shields and spears, but by the encouragement of noble words.

12. "Hear, O Israel, you are approaching the battle against your enemies today. Do not be fainthearted. Do not be afraid, or panic, or tremble before them, for your God is the one who goes with you, to fight for you against your enemies, and he will give you victory."

+13. The eloquent words that Jehoshaphat spoke encouraged everyone to be brave, and inspired boys to fight like men.

14. "When your God lets you capture the city, kill every

---

[19] *Penitence*

	man in it. You²⁰ may, however, take for yourselves the children, the livestock, and everything else in the city. You may use everything that belongs to your enemies."
+15.	"God has given it to you."
16.	So by fighting with their hands and praying to God in their hearts, the Jews killed more than 35,000.
17.	Jehoshaphat and his people went out to plunder the bodies and came away loaded with money, garments, and jewels stripped from the corpses--so much that it took them three days to cart it all away.
+18.	Then Jehoshaphat said, "Have you let all the women live?"
19.	"Kill them, so that they will not make you sin by teaching you to do all the disgusting things that they do in the worship of their gods."
20.	"Kill every woman who has had sexual intercourse, but keep alive for yourselves all the girls and all the women who are virgins."²¹
+21.	And behold, the word of the YAH-way came to Jehoshaphat, and said to him, "What are you doing?"
+22.	"All that I say, that you must do."
+23.	"But by these deeds thou hast given great occasion to My enemies to blaspheme against Me."
24.	"The arrogance of your heart has deceived you."
+25.	Jehoshaphat answered, "How shall we know the word which YAH-way has not spoken?"

---

[20] *Capture*
[21] *35000*

26. "Learn not the way of the heathen, but understandeth and knoweth me, that I am the YAH-way Who practices loving-kindness and righteousness in the earth."

27. "A bitter and hasty nation marches through the breadth of the earth, to possess dwelling places that are not theirs."[22]

28. "Wealth is deceitful. Greedy men are proud and restless--like death itself they are never satisfied. That is why they conquer nation after nation for themselves, that they might enlarge their territory."

+29. "O house of Israel, trust in Me. I am your possession, the God of Good."

30. "Be fearless, with integrity, in your stand for truth and honesty."

31. "The blameless will have a goodly inheritance. That is enough!"

+32. "Be content with this, and stay at home."

33. "Why stir up trouble that will only bring disaster on you and your people?"

34. "Make sure that you know what it is to serve me and what it is to serve earthly kingdoms."

35. "Nevertheless there are some good things about you, and you have tried to be faithful."[23]

36. "From this day forward I will bless you."

37. Then the realm of Jehoshaphat was quiet, and God gave him security on every side.

38. And Jehoshaphat grew old and was full of days, and he died.

---

[22] *Word*
[23] *Greedy*

Four--Jonah

+1. Then the Spirit of the YAH-way came upon Jonah.

2. One day YAH-way spoke to Jonah the son of Amittai, saying, "Arise, go unto Ninevah, that great city, and proclaim to it the message that I tell you."

3. But it displeased Jonah exceedingly, and he became angry.

+4. "It is twenty-five days' journey from here to there," he cried. "Why[24] should I go?"

+5. Then God put the answer into his mind.

6. "Know that I, YAH-way, have spoken. Rise and go. The word which I speak to you--that you shall do."

7. So Jonah arose, and went unto Ninevah.

+8. And as he went forth, thunder and rain filled the sky, not just once or twice, but many times.

+9. And he had to spend these nights in the cold--wet from the showers and huddled around a rock.

+10. When Jonah reached the city of Ninevah, he began to go into the city.

11. He walked for one day in the city. When he reached a certain place, he stopped for the night because the sun had set; and he took of the stones of that place, and put them for his pillows, and lay down to sleep.[25]

---

[24]*Ninevah*
[25]*Huddled*

12. But the next morning at dawn there came a great wind.

+13. From morning until noon, such a violent storm arose that the citizens of Ninevah were terrified and cried out for help, each one to his own god.

+14. And when some of the people saw Jonah, they said to him, "What do you mean, you sleeper? Arise, call upon your god! Perhaps your god will be concerned about us so that we will not perish."

15. "What is your occupation? And where do you come from?"

16. Like a man awakened from his sleep, Jonah answered them, "I am a Hebrew."

17. "I come to you from a distant land--Galilee."

18. "I come to you in the name of YAH-way, whom I fear."

19. "Take heed, all you people! On earth there is nothing like him."[26]

20. "Morning by morning, day by day, YAH-way speaks into my mind."

21. "Listen diligently to Me," my God tells me. "Salvation comes from the YAH-way. Not by might nor by power, but by My spirit you shall be safeguarded."

22. "Fear nothing. I'll protect you."

23. "But whoever will not hear My words will have a life filled with disgrace and contention."

24. One of the people spoke and said, "Can we find a shelter to give refuge and protection from the storm and the rain?"

---

[26]*Hebrew*

+25. So they found a house and entered in by the gates.

+26. Then they inquired further, and said to Jonah, "God has given you wisdom beyond your years, so explain to us what you mean, that YAH-way your God may show us the way in which we should walk and the thing we should do."[27]

27. Jonah said to them, "Alas! Alas! The people will labor in vain, and become exhausted who walk defiantly against the Almighty, running stubbornly against his holy Spirit."

28. "Present your case. Set forth your arguments. Bring in your idols. Let them come and do something; yes, do good or do evil."

+29. "Then we will know that they are gods!"

30. "But when I look, there is no counselor among them who, if I ask, can give me an answer. Behold, all of them are false; their works are worthless, their molten images are wind and emptiness."

+31. "He who chooses one of these chooses a delusion."

32. "You shall seek them and not find them. They are nothing at all--a nonexistent thing."

33. "But happy and blessed are the people whose god is the YAH-way."[28]

34. "For I will hold your right hand. Fear not. I will help you, if you listen," says the Holy One of Israel.

+35. While Jonah was speaking, the force and severity of the storm had diminished.

---

[27]*Contention*
[28]*Nonexistent*

36. And the people of Ninevah gave thanks for his words.

37. "Everything you have said makes good sense, and no one can argue with it."

38. Then all the people departed, each to his own home.

+39. Jonah went out west of the city and sat down.

40. And he prayed to YAH-way and said, "Ah, LORD, what shall I do now?"

+41. "Thank you. I remember My worthies. You may go home, Jonah."

42. "Because your heart was responsive and you humbled yourself when[29] you heard My words against this city and its people, I in turn have listened."

43. "You have taken some of the seed of a kingdom which shall never be destroyed, and planted it in a fertile field. That's enough."

+44. By the way that he came, by the same he returned, with the good hand of his God upon him.

Five--Mattathias

1. Then the Spirit of God came upon a priest of the Jehoiarib family named Mattathias, who settled in Modein.

2. Two years later, the wicked ruler Antiochus Epiphanes, son of King Antiochus the Third of Syria, sent a large army against the towns of Judea.

+3. Then he launched a fierce attack and issued a decree that all

---

[29]*Responsive*

the[30] people should abandon their own customs, adopt the official pagan religion, and offer sacrifices to idols.

4. All the Gentiles and even many of the Israelites submitted to this decree. But many people in Israel firmly resisted the king's decree.

5. When Mattathias saw all these terrible things, he said: "Why was I born? Must I sit here helpless while the city is surrendered into the hands of foreigners? Why should we go on living?"

6. In their grief, Mattathias and his sons tore their clothes, put on sackcloth, and continued in deep mourning.

7. The king's officials said to Mattathias, "You are a respected leader in this town, and you have the support of your sons and relatives. Why not be the first one here to do what the king has commanded? If you do, you and your sons will be honored with the title of 'Friends of the King,' and you will be rewarded with silver and gold and many gifts."

8. But Mattathias answered in a loud voice: "Although all the Gentiles[31] in the king's realm obey him, yet I and my sons and my kinsmen will keep to the covenant of our fathers."

9. Then Mattathias chose ambassadors and sent the following message to a group of Hasideans, valiant Israelites, at Beth Horon.

+10. "We have found a document reminding us that we are related and that both your families and ours are descended from Noah. We have written to renew our ties of brotherhood and friendship with you. We do not wish to become total strangers, and it has now been many years since our last communication."

---

[30] *Mattathias*
[31] *Sackcloth*

11.	"Throughout the years we have taken every opportunity, on our festival days and other suitable days, to remember you, as it is fitting and proper for brothers to do. We also are pleased that fame has come to you. Mercy and truth be with you."
12.	"We did not wish to trouble you or our other allies and friends, but we have had one series of troubles after another and have been under constant attack by surrounding nations."[32]
+13.	"If you come and help us, then we will come and help you at the time when you cry for help."
+14.	But the Hasideans scorned and ridiculed these messengers.
+15.	"What is this thing that you are doing?" the couriers asked. "Please let there be no strife between you and us, for we are brothers."
+16.	But the Hasideans would not go with them to help them.
+17.	The messengers left Beth Horon and went to report the news to Mattathias.
18.	Then Mattathias went through the town shouting, "Everyone who is faithful to the God of our fathers, follow me!"
19.	Thereupon he fled to the mountains, he and his sons. At that time also many of the Israelites went out to live in the wilderness, taking their children, their wives, and their livestock with them.[33]
20.	It was reported to the king that some men who had defied the king's command had gone out to the hiding places in the desert.

---

[32] *Ambassadors*
[33] *Strife*

21. A large force of soldiers pursued them, caught up with them, and prepared to attack.

22. "There is still time," they shouted out to the Jews. "Come out and obey the king's command, and we will spare your lives."

23. But they replied, "We will not come out."

24. The soldiers attacked them immediately, but the Jews did nothing to resist; they did not even throw stones or block the entrances to the caves where they were hiding.

25. They said, "We will all die with a clear conscience. Let heaven and earth bear witness that you are slaughtering us unjustly, that every Jewish family of every future generation in every province and every city should remember this day for all time to come."[34]

26. So the enemy attacked them and killed the men, their wives, their children, and their livestock. A thousand people died.

27. When Antiochus heard what happened, he was so dumbfounded and terribly shaken that he went to bed in a fit of deep depression. There he remained many days. Waves of despair swept over him. Finally he realized that he was going to die.

28. Not long after this, he died in misery and disgrace. His own death was unmourned. He was not given a funeral or even buried with his ancestors.

29. And it happened after this that, year by year, from east and west, from north and south, from sea to sea, and mountain to mountain, the land of Judea pined for good.

30. All the Jews that were in these nations feared YAH-way, but also served their idols; also their children and their children's children have continued doing as their fathers did, some of

---

[34] *Pursued*

them even to this day.[35]

Six--David....

+1. There was then no king in the land. But it came about that a man by the name of David soon became king.

+2. All Israel and Judah loved him, for he was a very good-looking man.

3. One day David met with a couple of counselors and they were speaking with him.

4. "How are you doing? Why do you look so worried today?" said one of the king's counselors.

5. David replied, "I was at rest in my house, and these were the visions of my head while on my bed. It is God who has dismayed me. Behold, I go forward but He is not there, and backward, but I cannot perceive Him. Should He come near me, I see Him not; should He pass by, I am not aware of Him."

6. At evening time, David came to his house.[36]

7. Then the king said to his servant, "Now bring me a musician."

+8. And it happened, as the musician played his harp, that the power of the YAH-way came upon the king.

9. And in his strength he struggled with God.

+10. He heard the sound of words, but he saw no visible likeness--only a voice: "The king who judges the poor

---
[35] *Dumbfounded*
[36] *Dismayed*

with truth and equity will establish his throne forever. If you are kind to these people, and please them, and speak good words to them, they will be your servants forever."

11. Suddenly an angel touched him.

12. Then David lifted his eyes and saw the angel of YAH-way standing between earth and heaven.

13. And David said to God, "Indeed, I am the one who has done very wickedly."[37]

+14. "For many years I have not trusted You or yearned for You with my whole heart, nor have I desired to know Your ways. For I was afraid of the anger and hot displeasure of all the nations who surround us."

+15. "In fear, I was prepared like a king poised to attack."

+16. "Blessed is Your advice and blessed are You, because You have kept me this day from coming to bloodshed and from defending myself with the lives of Your sheep. For what have they done wrong, that I should send them out to die for me?"

17. "From today on I will feed them and be their shepherd. I will make a covenant of peace with them. I will shepherd the flock with justice. No more will other nations conquer them. They shall live in safety and no one shall make them afraid."

18. "For the YAH-way will be our guide, the Prince of Peace."

19. And the Spirit of YAH-way came mightily upon David from that day forward.[38]

---

[37] *Establish*
[38] *Yearned*

+20. And he proclaimed to the people, "I will surely not take what is yours for burnt offerings with that which costs me nothing. I will not take anything at all that is yours, lest you should say, 'our gifts have made David rich.' And if I ever repay evil to him who was at peace with me, or if we ever plunder our enemy shamefully, let them pursue me and overtake me; yes, let them trample my life, and lay my honor in the dust."

21. And they whispered to each other, "God bless King David. In him there is found something good."

22. But there was a man whose name was Kish, a wealthy and influential man, and he had a son whose name was Saul, a choice and handsome young man. There was not a more handsome person than he among the children of Israel.

+23. One day Saul confessed his desire, "If only I were appointed king in the land instead of David!"

+24. So Saul mobilized an army to besiege David and his men.[39]

25. And the conspiracy grew strong. But David learned of Saul's plan.

26. "O YAH-way," David said, "I have heard that Saul plans to come and destroy me. What shall I do?"

+27. Shortly afterwards, some people went to David and said, "Is Saul not hiding in strongholds in the woods, in the hill of Hachilah, which is on the south of Jeshimon?"

28. And David said: "Please go and find out for sure, and see the place where his hideout is, and who has seen him there. For I am told that he is very crafty. Be sure to bring back a report to me right away. Then I will go, and if he is still in the region, I will hunt him down."

---

[39] *Shamefully*

29. So they arose and went to the southern part of the Judean wilderness.

30. Then the men of David returned, and said to him, "Hurry! We have found him. YAH-way has put your enemy into your hand, that you may do to him as it seems good to you."[40]

31. So David arose and came to the place where Saul had encamped; and there Saul lay sleeping within the camp, with his spear stuck in the ground by his head. So David took the spear and the jug of water by Saul's head; and no man saw it or knew it or awoke.

+32. He climbed the mountain slope opposite the camp until he was at a safe distance.

33. Then he shouted to Saul, "The YAH-way will decide between us. May he punish you for your action against me, but I will never harm you."

+34. "And now see where your spear is, and the jug of water that was by your head. Behold, I have taken them."

35. Then Saul knew David's voice, and said, "David, is that you?"

36. And David said, "It is my voice."

37. Then Saul said, "Because you have spared my life tonight, I will not try to harm you again. Surely I have acted like a fool and have erred[41] greatly. You are a better man than I am, for you have repaid me good for evil. For if a man finds his enemy, will he let him get away safely? Therefore, may the YAH-way reward you with good for what you have done to me this day."

---

[40] *Hideout*
[41] *Saul*

+38. Then Saul said to David, "Behold now, I perceive that you are a holy man of God in whom I find no fault."

39. So David went on his way home.

40. And as he went, he said, "YAH-way is God in heaven and on earth. There is no other like you. I am your servant and your son, who desires to do justice and righteousness. Your gentleness has made me great."

Seven--Daniel

+1. Some time after the days that David was king in the land, there was[42] another man who was named Daniel.

2. And he lay down on his bed, and turned away his face, and would eat no food.

3. "In those days I, Daniel, had been mourning for three entire weeks. I ate no pleasant food, no meat or wine came into my mouth, nor did I anoint myself at all, till three whole weeks were fulfilled."

4. "Then behold, a hand touched me and set me trembling on my knees and the palms of my hands, and a voice was heard in my ear."

5. "O Daniel, man greatly beloved, I will teach you the good and the right way."

+6. "Only revere Me and serve Me in truth with all your heart."

---

[42]*Righteousness*

7.   Then I said to one of my servants, "Please bring me a morsel of bread in your hand. And please bring me a little water in a cup, that I may drink."[43]

8. And he revived and felt his strength returning.

9. Now it came to pass after many days that he brought a great assembly together, then spoke to them these words.

10.   "Hear, all you peoples! Listen, O earth, and all that is in it!"

11.   "All of you are children of the Most High."

+12.   "Did not the same One form us all within our mothers?"

13.   "Now therefore hearken, O Israel. Listen to me and act! Success against one's own people is the worst kind of failure."

14.   "Therefore when you see people who have great pain because of hunger, set food and water before them, that they may eat and drink."

15. And so it happened that Israel clothed all who were naked among them, dressed them and gave them sandals, gave them food and drink, and anointed them. In the land, those who gathered much did not have too[44] much, and those who gathered less did not have too little. Each gathered according to his need.

+16. One day two young prostitutes came to Daniel to have an argument settled.

+17.   One of them said, "We have heard of the soundness and maturity of your judgment, and that light and understanding and excellent wisdom are found in you, and that the spirit of the holy gods is in you."

---

[43] *Daniel*
[44] *Success*

18. "Sir, we live in the same house, just the two of us, and recently I had a baby. When it was three days old, this woman's baby was born too. But her baby died during the night when she rolled over on it in her sleep and smothered it. Then she got up in the night and took my son from beside me while I was asleep, and laid her dead child in my arms and took mine to sleep beside her. And in the morning when I tried to feed my baby it was dead! But when it became light outside, I saw that it wasn't my son at all."

19. Then the other woman interrupted, "It certainly was her son, and the[45] living child is mine."

20. "No," the first woman said, "the dead one is yours and the living one is mine."

21. And so they argued back and forth.

22. Daniel answered and said: "This one says, 'My son is alive and your son is dead,' while that one says, 'No! Your son is dead and mine is alive.'"

23. Then he said, "All right, bring me a sword."

24. And when it was brought, he said, "Cut the living child in two and give each woman half of it."

25. Then the woman whose son was living spoke, for she yearned with compassion for her son.

26. And she said, "O my lord, give her the living child. Don't kill him!"[46]

27. But the other said, "It shall be neither mine nor yours; go on and cut it in two."

---

[45] *Baby*
[46] *Half*

28. Daniel replied, "Give the living child to the first woman, and by no means slay it; she is its mother."

+29. Word of Daniel's decision spread quickly, and all the people were awed, because they perceived that the wisdom of God was in him to administer truly just judgments.

30. Then the Spirit of the YAH-way spoke through me to me, in the sound of a gentle whisper: "I am YAH-way, that is My name; I am he who created the heavens and stretched them out, who spread out the earth and all that comes out of it, who gives breath to its people, and life to those who walk on it: I will not give my glory to another; I will not share my praise with carved idols."

31. "I, YAH-way, have called you for the victory of justice, to demonstrate my righteousness. I have grasped you by the hand. Through you I will make a covenant with all peoples; through you I[47] will bring light to the nations. You will open the eyes of the blind, bring out prisoners from the dungeon, and set free those who sit in dark prisons."

+32. Then Daniel bowed down on the ground, and put his face between his knees, in deep humility, beholding, regarding, and wondering at these words.

33. Inasmuch as an excellent spirit, knowledge, understanding, interpreting dreams, solving riddles, and explaining enigmas were found in this Daniel, he was faithful as the YAH-way's servant until the day of his death.

Eight--Solomon

1. Then Solomon sat on the throne as king, and all Israel obeyed him.

---

[47] *Administer*

2. Now Solomon was strengthened in his kingdom, and YAH-way was[48] with him and exalted him exceedingly.

3. And God said to Solomon: "Go up to Jerusalem, for Jerusalem is the place I have chosen for you to live. You shall make it the most beautiful city in all the world, and take many out of all your tribes to live with you, so that the Israelites may dwell in a place of their own and move no more."

+4. Four months later, Solomon set a time for his departure, then traveled to Jerusalem.

+5. Three days after his arrival, in the middle of the night he got up and went out into the city, taking a few of his companions with him. (He had not yet told anyone about the plans for Jerusalem which God had put into his heart.)

6. "I was mounted on my donkey and the others were on foot. I went out by the Valley Gate to the Jackal's Well and to the Dung Gate, and I inspected the walls of Jerusalem which were broken down and its gates which had been destroyed by fire. Then I went on to the Fountain[49] Gate and to the King's Pool."

7. "Then I said, 'You see how Jerusalem lies desolate, and its gates are burned with fire. Let's rebuild the city walls.'"

8. "And I told the men with me about the desire God had put into my heart."

9. "They responded, 'If it seems good to you, and if it is of the YAH-way our God, we will do it.'"

+10. The next morning, Solomon visited the mayor of Jerusalem.

+11. Now when Solomon had finished telling the mayor

---

[48]*Dungeon*
[49]*Jerusalem*

about his heart's desire to rebuild the wall of Jerusalem and create a city of exquisite beauty, the mayor said, "Go in peace, and may the God of Israel give you what you desire. Whatever seems good to you and your brethren, do it according to the will of your God. And I will watch to see that you are not hindered."[50]

+12. So Solomon was encouraged, as the hand of YAH-way was upon him.

13. So it was, when the Jews were ready to begin, they cast lots for their duties, whether they were young or old, experts or beginners.

14. Then Solomon spoke: "Be strong and do not let your hands be weak."

15. And all the people that were with him did for him just as he had commanded them.

16. So the workmen labored, with the voice of thanksgiving. Thus they did day by day. And the task of restoration progressed under their hands.

17. Now it happened, when Sanballat, Tobiah, the Arabs, the Ammonites, and the Ashdodites heard that the walls of Jerusalem were being restored and the gaps were beginning to be closed, that they became very angry, and all of them conspired together to come and attack Jerusalem and create confusion.

+18. And Sanballat and Tobiah mocked the Jews and despised them, and said,[51] "What are these feeble Jews doing? Will they revive the stones from the heaps of rubbish?"

19. Solomon replied, "We are the servants of the God of heaven and earth."

---

[50] *Exquisite*
[51] *Encouraged*

20.   "All inhabitants of the world and dwellers on the earth, hear now my words: Jerusalem shall be called the City of Truth. For the sake of my brethren and companions, I will now say, Peace be within you, Peace be within your walls. From this time forth, I will seek your good."

21. After fifty-two days of work the entire wall was finished. Everyone who was there joined in worship, the people sang praise to the YAH-way, and the musicians began to play the trumpets and all the other instruments.

22. The leaders settled in Jerusalem, and the rest of the people drew lots to choose one family out of every ten to go and live in the holy city of Jerusalem, while the rest were to live in the other cities and towns.

23. And Solomon had twelve governors over all Israel, who provided food for the king and his household; each one made provision for one month of the[52] year. Solomon's supplies for each day were 195 bushels of fine flour, 390 bushels of meal, 10 oxen from the fattening pens, 20 pasture-fed cattle, 100 sheep, and, from time to time, deer, gazelles, roebucks, and plump fowl. And these governors, each man in his month, provided food for King Solomon and for all who came to King Solomon's table. There was no lack in their supply.

24. Throughout the lifetime of Solomon, all of Judah and Israel lived in peace and safety; and each family had its own home and garden.

25.   Solomon said, "Now YAH-way my God has given me rest on every side, so that there is neither adversary nor misfortune."[53]

---

[52]*Truth*
[53]*Table*

Poetry (Po)

One

1. And the land was broad, quiet, and peaceful.

2. "Trust in the YAH-way, and do good; dwell in the land, and feed on YAH-way's faithfulness. Delight yourself also in God, and the YAH-way shall give you the desires of your heart."

3. "Every word of the YAH-way is pure; God is a shield to those who put their trust in the YAH-way."

4. "All YAH-way's words are right, and all God's work is done in truth. The YAH-way loves whatever is just and good."

5. "Full of wisdom and perfect in beauty, the earth is full of the goodness of God."

6. "Open to me the gates of righteousness; I will go through them."

7. "All the forces of nature fight on behalf of those who are just."[1]

8. "Mercy and truth have met together; righteousness and peace have kissed each other. Truth shall spring out of the earth, and righteousness shall look down from heaven."

9. "And YAH-way will repay each man for doing good and being loyal."

10. "God's way is unerring, to light the way they should go for all those who take refuge in him."

---

[1] *Delight*

11.	"Be careful to seek out all the instructions of the YAH-way."
12.	"Whatever is commanded by the God of heaven, let it diligently be done."
+13.	"Men and women, seek Me and live, all who are of a willing heart."
14.	"YAH-way your God loves you, and is faithful for a thousand generations toward those who love and obey him."
15.	"May you always be blessed with good health and happiness, and may the YAH-way show lovingkindness and truth to you."[2]
16.	"Yet brace yourself like a man. When the sun arises, and man goes forth to his work and remains at his task until evening, as each day may require, be not far from Me, for trouble is near."
17.	Then an angel said, "Lift your eyes now, and see a vision of a bushel basket filled with the iniquity of the people prevailing everywhere throughout all the earth."
18.	The basket had a lid made of lead. And behold, the leaden cover was lifted, and there in the basket sat a woman!
19.	Then the angel said, "This is Wickedness!"
20.	But the people will shout, "Beautiful, beautiful!"
+21.	Then the angel pushed her back into the basket and replaced the cover.
22.	And the angel cried out, "To Babylonia!--where they will build a temple for her. When the temple is finished, she

---

[2] *Generations*

	will be set there on her own pedestal to be worshiped."³
23.	"Have courage! Don't be afraid. Speak the truth to one another. And the people of Jerusalem and Judah will be blessed."
+24.	But the people stubbornly refused to listen. They closed their minds and made their hearts as hard as rock.
25.	They abandoned the YAH-way their God, and embraced other gods and served them.
+26.	Nevertheless, even though their heart was not right or sincere, from the greatest to the least of them, they continued to flatter YAH-way with their mouths and lie to him with their tongues and tried to deceive him with friendly greetings and sworn pledges.
27.	It was the beginning of sin on the earth.⁴

Two--Susanna

+1.	In Jerusalem there lived a man named Joakim, who was married to Susanna.
+2.	Susanna's beautiful face and attractive figure were as lovely as the light from the sacred lampstand in the Temple.
3.	Her husband Joakim was very wealthy. Everyone who had a legal case to present would go to Joakim's house, where two judges held court. Every day at noon, when all the people left for lunch, Susanna used to take a walk in the gardens. The two judges began to lust for her. Day by day they watched eagerly for her. They became so obsessed with their desire for her that they lost interest both in prayer and

---

³*Pedestal*
⁴*Closed*

in their responsibility as judges. Each was ashamed to admit his lust. They each wanted Susanna, but neither told the other how he felt.

+4. Their loins trembled continually. They hotly pursued her with their whole desire, and wanted her above everything else.

5. It enveloped them in flames, yet they did not realize; it burned them,[5] but they did not take it to heart.

+6. Their hearts were smooth, false, divided and deceitful.

7. One day, while they were waiting for the right moment, she entered the garden as usual. She decided to bathe, for the weather was warm.

8. So she said to her servants, "Bring me some bath oil and some perfume, and lock the gates."

9. As soon as the servants had left, the two judges jumped out from their hiding place, and said, "Turn back, my daughter, and draw near."

10. Then she said, "What are you doing? Where did you come from? Leave me alone."

11. "Look," they said, "if you are so minded, consider and behold our affliction, and please rescue us."

12. "What is your request? And why have I found favor in your eyes,[6] that you should take notice of me?"

+13. "We think you may be able to help us."

14. "Ask! What shall I give you?"

15. The two old men hurried to her. "The gates are locked and no one will see us. We are burning to

---

[5] *Susanna*
[6] *Bathe*

have sex with you, so give us what we want. If you refuse, we will go to court and swear that we saw you send your servants away, so that you could be alone with a young man."

16. Susanna groaned. Through her tears she looked up to heaven, for she trusted in YAH-way wholeheartedly.

+17. She wanted to cry for help, but she did not do so.

+18. "If it is a matter of strength, indeed they are strong; I am innocent and faithful, but who will give me justice in the court?"

19. "Weeds were wrapped around my head. The earth with its bars closed[7] behind me forever."

20. "If YAH-way would make windows in heaven, could this thing be?"

+21. Susanna heard a voice of One speaking, "It shall not be."

22. Being awake and aware, she spoke: "Pause and wonder! Why do you do such things? Men of understanding, as the YAH-way lives, and as your soul lives, will there not be peace and truth? Everyone who is born is caught in the web of sin. There is no one in the present generation who has not sinned. Yet from days of old, from that time even until now, men live by the fruit of their conduct and their actions. They are joined one to another; they stick together and cannot be parted. Remember this, a lying tongue hates those who are crushed by it. If it be so, our God's occasion to test me, while this is being done by your hands, I will strip and go naked."

+23. The two men who had wanted her just a few minutes ago,

---

[7] *Innocent*

now conceived an intense dislike for her, because they thought she had gone mad.[8]

+24. Then she said, "YAH-way in his holy knowledge knows full well that I could have escaped from you, yet I gladly suffer with joy in my soul because of my devotion to God. I came naked from my mother's womb, and I shall have nothing when I die. YAH-way gives and the YAH-way takes. Blessed be God. Hear Thou from heaven Thy dwelling place, and forgive. Deal with each person according to his conduct, for You alone know the hearts of men."

+25. In all of this, Susanna did not blame the YAH-way, nor did she say anything disrespectful.

26. One of the judges walked back and forth, thoroughly bewildered! The other sat down astonished.

+27. Then Susanna said to them, "Rest and be still! May the YAH-way deal kindly with you."

+28. The first man stopped pacing and said, "Susanna, you are righteous, more than we knew. And now, O our God, what shall we say after this?"[9]

+29. The second old man exclaimed, "O lying tongue, what shall be your fate?" And he prayed that he might die, and said, "It is enough! YAH-way, now that I am old and my hair is gray, take my life, for the ways in which we walk are vile."

30. After that, the men left the garden.

31. Then Susanna was overjoyed and prayed, "I have escaped by the skin of my teeth. How I wish that someone would remember my words and record them in a book! As long as I live, while I have my being, I will sing praise to my God."

---

[8] *Pause*
[9] *Forgive*

Three--Joebh

1. Living in the land of Uz, around this time, was a man named Joebh, and he was blameless and upright.

2. He had seven sons and three daughters and many servants. His sons[10] used to take turns holding feasts in their homes.

3. One day a messenger came to Joebh and said, "The oxen were plowing and the donkeys were grazing nearby, and the Sabeans attacked and carried them off."

4. And after this, another messenger came and said, "Fire fell from the sky and burned up the sheep and the servants."

5. After these events, still another messenger rushed in and said, "Your sons and daughters were feasting and drinking when suddenly a mighty wind swept in and struck the four corners of the house. It collapsed on them and they are dead."

+6. Joebh's flesh was in pain when he heard this, and his soul within him mourned.

+7. Then Joebh was afflicted with painful sores from the soles of his feet to the top of his head.[11]

8. And Joebh spoke, and said: "May the day perish on which I was born, and the night when I was conceived. May it be blotted off the calendar, never again to be counted among the days of the month of that year. Oh, may that night be barren! May the stars of its morning be dark, and not see the eyelids of the dawn. I wish I had died in my mother's womb. Is life so great?"

---

[10] *Uz*
[11] *Joebh*

+9. "Most men have not enough. Hungry and thirsty, their souls faint within them. All his days a man eats in darkness, and he has much sorrow and sickness and anger. What profit has he who has labored for the wind? I have chosen the way of truth, and now in my day of adversity, must I not speak and give my complaint?"

10. "These people have no master; they are as sheep that have no shepherd."

+11. "Where is the YAH-way, the God of Daniel and Noah?"

12. "Where is He who put His Holy Spirit within them?"

13. "I am the most ignorant of men. I have not learned wisdom, nor have I[12] knowledge of the Holy One. Who has ascended into heaven, or descended? Who has gathered the wind in His fists? Who has bound the waters in a garment? What is His name, and what is His Son's name? Do you know?"

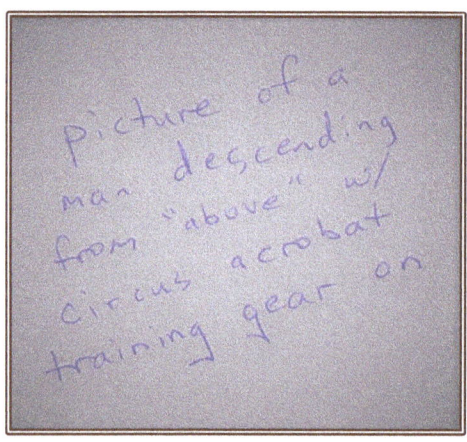

14. "Arise, O God, plead Your own cause; remember how the foolish man taunts You daily."

---

[12]*Ignorant*

15. "And as for me, why should I suffer? My hands are free from violence, and my prayer is sincere. Tell me, what have I done wrong? Help me!"

16. "My friends scorn me; my eyes pour out tears. My breath is offensive to my wife. My acquaintances have cast off all restraint in my presence. They despise me and won't come near me, and don't mind spitting in my face. My heart is broken. Depression haunts my days. My weary nights are filled with pain as though something were relentlessly gnawing at my bones."

+17. "Also, my eyes torment my soul at the sight of all the daughters of my city. I see them with my eyes but I cannot eat from there. If anyone[13] tries to buy love with his wealth, contempt is all he will get. I request of you, O daughters of the earth, that you do not stir up affection until it pleases."

18. "A foolish woman is clamorous; she is simple, and knows nothing. For she sits at the door of her house, and calls out to people passing by, 'Whoever is naive, turn in here.'"

19. "But here is what I want to see: let justice flow like a river and righteousness like an ever-flowing stream."

20. Then Joebh continued and said, "My God, my Holy One, all mankind wait for You, that You may give them their food in due season. What You give them they gather in; You open Your hand, they are filled with good. You hide Your face, they are troubled; You take away their breath, they die and return to their dust. You send forth Your Spirit, they are created; and You renew the face of the earth.

---

[13] *Fists*

21.	"These receive Your blessings but they deny You."[14]
22.	"They are terrible and dreadful; they think their justice and dignity proceed only from themselves."
+23.	"To me their behavior is as foul as the filthy rags of a menstruous woman."
24.	"Truly the hearts of the sons of men are full of evil, and insanity is in their minds throughout their lives, and afterward they join the dead. But for him who is among the living, there is hope--even a live dog is better off than a dead lion! For the living know they will die, but the dead know nothing."
25.	"There is hope for a tree, if it is cut down, that it will sprout again, and that its tender shoots will not cease. Though its root may grow old in the earth, and its stump may die in the ground, yet at the scent of water it will bud and bring forth branches like a plant. But man dies and is laid away; indeed, he breathes his last and where is he? Like a cloud that fades and is gone, so he who goes down to the grave does not come up."[15]
26.	"You shall be no more; though you are sought for, you will never be found again."
+27.	Then an angel talked with Joebh, and said to him, "O watcher of men, you son of a bitch, how long will you be angry? How long will your jealousy burn? Collect your thoughts. Unbend yourself, and listen."
+28.	Then the angel said, "Even you were as one of them. For how can any man at all be righteous before God, or pure who is born of a woman? When God sends you something good, you welcome it. Will you not also accept adversity in its time?"

---

[14]*Clamorous*
[15]*Filthy*

+29. Then Joebh set his countenance in a stare until he was ashamed; and the man of God wept.

+30. Then Joebh replied and said, "I will be His son, and He shall be my Father."

31. "Praise YAH! Praise him from the skies! Praise him, all his angels, sun and moon, and all you twinkling stars."[16]

32. "The 'month' is named after the marvelous moon. Its light grows full and then grows dim, shining out in the dome of the sky."

33. "Praise Him, you heavens of heavens. Let them praise the name of the YAH-way, for He commanded and they were created. He set them in place for ever and ever. Praise YAH-way from the earth, you great sea creatures and all ocean depths, lightning and hail, stormy winds, hills and mountains, fruit trees and forests, the wild animals and cattle, the snakes and birds, kings and all people, princes and judges of the earth, young men and maidens, old men and children. Let them praise the name of God."

34. "Deep calls to deep in the roar of your waterfalls; all your waves and breakers have swept over me."

+35. "Therefore I retract my complaints, and I repent in dust and ashes. Blessed be the one who took notice of me."

+36. Now while Joebh was praying, and while he was confessing, weeping, and bowing down, a very large congregation of men, women, and children[17] assembled to him from Israel; and the people joined him in weeping.

---

[16] *Bitch*
[17] *Confessing*

37. And so it was that the YAH-way restored Joebh's losses. Indeed YAH-way gave Joebh twice as much as he had before. And in all the land there were no other girls so fair and lovely as the daughters of Joebh.

Four--Ruth

1. The name of the youngest of these daughters was Naomi.

2. A man named Elimelech, who lived in Bethlehem, joined together with Naomi, and they had two sons, Mahlon and Chilion. Because of a famine, they went to live for a while in the country of Moab. Some time after their arrival on the Moabite plateau, Elimelech died, and she was left with her two sons, who married Moabite women, one named Orpah, the other Ruth.

3. After they had lived there about ten years, both men died, so that[18] Naomi was left alone, without her husband or sons.

4. Then she decided to return to Bethlehem.

5. And Naomi said to her two daughters-in-law, "How are you, my daughters? Do all that is in your heart. But I think it is better for you to return to your own people. And may the YAH-way deal kindly with you."

6. But Ruth replied, "Don't make me leave you, for I want to go wherever you go, and where you stay I will stay. Your people shall be my people, and your God, my God. May YAH-way do terrible things to me if I allow anything but death to separate us. Where you die I will die, and there I will be buried."

+7. "Indeed, let YAH-way tie you and me together

---

[18]*Ruth*

forever."

8. So Naomi returned from Moab accompanied by Ruth, arriving in Bethlehem as the barley harvest was beginning.[19]

9. Now Naomi had a relative there who belonged to the family of her husband Elimelech. His name was Boaz, a man of great wealth.

10. And Naomi said to Ruth, "You will listen, my daughter, will you not? My daughter, shall I not seek security for you, that it may be well with you?"

+11. And she said to her, "Go to the field, my daughter, and glean among the ears of grain after him in whose sight you might find favor."

12. So Ruth went out to the fields.

13. And behold, Boaz came from town; and he said to the reapers, "Whose young woman is this?"

14. And the servant who was in charge of the reapers answered, "It is the Moabite maiden, who came back with Naomi from the country of Moab."

15. Then Boaz said to Ruth, "You shall stay close by my young men. Indeed, I have commanded the servants not to molest you."[20]

16. And he said to his men, "Let her gather grain even among the sheaves, and do not insult her. Besides that, also let some grain from the bundles fall purposely for her."

+17. So Ruth gleaned in the field until evening. Then she threshed the barley she had gathered, and it amounted to over half a bushel. She carried it back to town, and at mealtime Ruth and her mother-in-law ate until they were

---

[19] *Barley*
[20] *Boaz*

satisfied, and they had some left over.

18. And Ruth told her mother-in-law everything that Boaz had done for her.

19. "This is wonderful!" Naomi exclaimed. "It is good for you to go out with his young people until the end of the harvest, and that you don't go into any other fields."

20. So Ruth worked with them and gathered grain until all the barley had been harvested.

21. One day Naomi said to Ruth, "Is not Boaz a kinsman of ours? Now listen. This evening he will be threshing the barley. So wash yourself,[21] put on some perfume, and get dressed in your best clothes. Then go to the threshing-floor, but don't let him see you until he has finished his supper. Then it shall be, when he lies down, you shall go in and lie down; and he will tell you what you should do."

22. So she went down to the threshing-floor that night and followed her mother-in-law's instructions. After Boaz had finished a good meal, he lay down very contentedly beside a heap of grain and went to sleep. Then Ruth came softly, lifted the covers and lay down at his feet. During the night he woke up suddenly, turned over, and was surprised.

23. "Who are you?" he asked.

24. "It's Ruth, sir," she answered. "I will do whatever you say."

25. "My daughter, do not fear. What do you desire? I will listen, for I believe that you are a virtuous woman."

26. Then Ruth said, "Please marry me. Because you are a close relative, you are responsible for taking care of

---

[21] *Wonderful*

me."²²

27. "Stay here tonight," he exclaimed. "Lie down until the morning. I will satisfy your needs, as surely as the YAH-way lives!"

28. In the morning she got up before it was light enough for her to be seen, because Boaz did not want anyone to know that she had been there.

29. When she came home, her mother-in-law said, "How did it go?"

30. And Ruth told her.

31. Then Naomi said, "Wait, my daughter, until you find out what happens. For the man will not rest until the matter is settled today."

32. That afternoon Boaz took ten men of the elders of the city, and said, "Sit down here." So they sat down. And Boaz said to the elders and to all the people, "You are witnesses this day that I have acquired as my wife Ruth the Moabite, the widow of Mahlon."

33. And all the people said, "May your lovingkindness be famous in Bethlehem."²³

+34. So Boaz took Ruth and she became his wife; and when he went in to her, God enabled her to conceive, and she gave birth to a daughter. And they named her Abishag.

+35. And the women of the city said to Ruth, "Bless YAH-way who has given you this little child; may she be famous in Israel, and also be to you a restorer of life and a comfort in your old age."

---

²² *Surprised*
²³ *Satisfy*

Five--Abishag

1. And then there was the king, Hezekiah, who ruled in Jerusalem.

2. When Hezekiah was seventy-five years old, his servants covered him with blankets, but he could not keep warm.

3. Hezekiah turned his face to the wall and prayed, "As for me, my prayer is to You, O God. In the multitude of Your mercy, deliver me out of the mire, and let me not sink; let not the floodwater overflow me, nor let the[24] deep swallow me up, or the pit close its mouth over me."

4. "The cure for this," his servants said to him, "is to find a young virgin to be your concubine and nurse. She will lie in your arms and take care of you."

+5. "For the effect of a maiden on a man is too wonderful to understand."

6. So they searched for a beautiful girl throughout all the territory of Israel, and found Abishag, and brought her to the king. She was now seventeen years old.

+7. "The woman who is coming to your house will help you," one of Hezekiah's servants said.

+8. Now it was so, when she came to him, that the king said to her, "If you have come to me in friendship to help me, my heart will be united with yours."

9. And she attended to the king and took care of him, but he did not[25] have sexual intercourse with her.

10. One day Hezekiah said to her, "I am now about eighty years old. Can I discern between the good

---

[24] *Abishag*
[25] *Nurse*

	and bad? Can I hear any longer the voice of singing men and singing women?"
11.	"Yet I remember one time in my life: a long time ago I had a friend whose name was Jonathan."
+12.	"At the time when I first met him, women had not been near either of us for about three days. We were in the midst of a battle campaign. Our bodies were filled with the desire to embrace the bosom of a woman."
13.	"Then Jonathan said, 'You know, I love women. Nevertheless, a woman jealous of another woman causes heartache and grief. Her tongue lashes out at everyone.'"
14.	"'Yes, you are right,' I said. 'But pleasant words are a honeycomb, sweet to the soul and healing to the bones.'"[26]
+15.	"We talked for hours on the hills of the camp, and we kissed one another, and we wept together."
16.	"Then Jonathan said, 'May the YAH-way be between you and me, and between your descendants and my descendants, forever.'"
17.	"He and I stayed close and helped each other for many years, and our hearts were as though they were joined together. When he was very old, and before his death, I said to Jonathan, 'My brother, you have been very pleasant to me. Your love to me was more wonderful than the love of women.'"
18.	When King Hezekiah had finished speaking, Abishag spoke.
+19.	"My lord, you have strengthened me with your sincerity and truthfulness, and now I will tell you the truth. I have met a handsome person, and I love

---

[26] *Bodies*

	him as deeply as the covenant of brotherhood which you have just described."
20.	"Why didn't you tell me this before? Better is an open rebuke than a[27] love that remains hidden."
21.	"I feared your judgment."
+22.	"I would not restrain you from having a husband. There once was a man all alone; he had neither son nor brother. There was no end to his working, yet his eyes were not content with his wealth. 'For whom am I toiling,' he asked, 'and why am I depriving myself of enjoyment?' This is a miserable way to live."
+23.	Then the king also said, "One thing else I will say: Like a youthful woman, you will perhaps continue to behave in this manner--with the merciful you will show yourself merciful; with a blameless man you will show yourself blameless; with the sincere you will show yourself sincere; and with the devious you will show yourself shrewd. So judge for yourself which are more desirable and valuable, common things or rare things?"
24.	She answered, "Lord and master, the common things are cheap; it is the rare things that are valuable."[28]
25.	"All right," he replied, "so draw the logical conclusion: the person who has what is scarce has more reason to be pleased than the person who has what is plentiful. May YAH-way grant that you find rest in the house of your husband."
+26.	On the day of their wedding, all the people danced with all their might, with rejoicing and singing, to honor God. The singers played loudly on musical instruments, with song and

---

[27] *Deeply*
[28] *Hidden*

lyres and harps and tambourines and cymbals and trumpets, to raise sounds of joy. Everyone who wished to do so, whose hearts were stirred by the Spirit of YAH-way, joined with them.

Six--Sarah....

+1. Then Abishag gave birth to a daughter and named her Sarah. And she grew up into a young woman.

2. Sarah was in good health but not as comely as her mother.[29]

3. She had been engaged to seven husbands already, but not one of them had made it to that day of joy and feasting.

4. One day Sarah was so depressed that she burst into tears and went upstairs determined to hang herself. But she reconsidered, saying to herself, "No, I won't do it!"

5. Then Sarah stood by the window, raised her arms in prayer, and said, "God of mercy, worthy of our praise, blessed are you, O YAH-way. May all your creation praise you forever. And now, I look to you for help. The spirit of a man will sustain him in sickness, but who can bear a broken spirit? Speak the word and set me free from this life. I have already lost seven husbands, so why should I live any longer? But if it is not your will to take my life, at least show mercy to me."

+6. That same day in the city of Ecbatana, it happened that a man named Tobit called to his son Tobias, and said to him, "Do you know the way to Jerusalem? We have many of our kindred in that city, and I want you to go find a damsel to marry."[30]

---

[29] *Plentiful*
[30] *Sarah*

7. Tobit continued, "Be on your guard, son, against every form of immorality, and above all, marry a woman of the lineage of your forefathers. Do not be so proud-hearted toward your kinsmen, the sons and daughters of your people, as to refuse to take a wife for yourself from among them."

8. Then Tobias prepared for his journey.

9. As he was almost ready to leave, Tobit said, "The evil impulse within us has grown and it has led us away from God's ways. Listen to me. Don't be controlled by your lust; keep your passions in check. Prepare your outside work on the land, make it fit for yourself in the field; and afterward build your house. May the YAH-way bless and protect you. May the YAH-way shine upon and enlighten you, and be gracious to you. May the YAH-way look on you with favor and give you peace. Have a safe journey."

10. So Tobias left home for Jerusalem.

+11. At the very moment that Tobit went back into his house from sending[31] forth his son, Sarah was coming down the stairs in her house in Jerusalem.

12. In the midst of his trip a certain woman met him; she was dressed like a prostitute.

+13. She stopped him and propositioned him to sleep with her.

14. "How much will you pay me?" she asked.

+15. Tobias replied, "Peace and greetings. You are very desirable, but I will not enter into you today in this place, for a man of God is an honorable man."

16. She said, "What do you have against me, man of

---
[31]*Tobit*

God? Did you come to remind me of my sin?"

17. "No," he said. "May YAH-way be gracious to you."

+18. Thus Tobias continued on his way to Jerusalem.[32]

+19. When he reached the city, he said, "O YAH-way, the God of my father Tobit, please grant me success today, and show me your lovingkindness. Here I am at the well where the young women of the city will be coming to get water. May it be that you will choose a wife from one of them for me."

+20. And it came about, before he had finished his prayer, that behold, Sarah came out with her jar on her shoulder. And she went down to the well, filled her water jar, and came up.

+21. The man stood gazing at her in silence. Her sad and unpretentious demeanor grabbed hold of his heart.

22. "Whose daughter are you, and why is thy spirit so sad?"

23. She told him, and they discovered that they were indeed of the same family.

+24. Their mutual affection grew quickly, and a successful marriage in Jerusalem was not long following.[33]

25. Their fathers and their mothers all went to the wedding celebration, and Tobit said to Tobias and Sarah, "Two are better than one, because they have a good reward for their labor. For if they fall, one will lift up his companion. But woe to him who is alone when he falls, for he has no one to help him up. Again, if two lie down together, they will keep warm; but how can one be warm alone? Though one may be overpowered by another, two can withstand him. And a threefold cord is not quickly

---

[32] *Honorable*
[33] *Unpretentious*

broken. A man, a woman, and the YAH-way is a strong fortress. May the words that you speak in your bedroom be sincere and all true and may they tie together your hearts forever."

26. And they went forth to live and work in the town of Ephraim, and they had a daughter and gave the name of Esther to her.

Seven--Esther

1. When Esther was sixteen, an edict came from the king of Persia that King Xerxes was looking in all the provinces of his realm for young[34] virgins to add to his royal harem.

2. For the king was furious, and his anger burned within him, when Queen Vashti had disobeyed one of his commands.

3. "Let the young lady who pleases the king be queen in place of Vashti," some of the king's advisers had suggested.

4. So it was, as a result of the king's decree, Esther was brought to the king's harem at Shushan Palace, along with many other young girls.

+5. And Sarah and Tobias lifted up their voices and wept when their daughter was taken away from them.

+6. And Sarah especially was in bitterness of soul, and prayed to the YAH-way and wept in anguish.

+7. Then Tobias her husband said to her, "Sarah, why do you weep? Why do you not eat? And why is your heart still grieved? Is not my constant love worth anything to thee?"[35]

---

[34] *Esther*
[35] *Vashti*

8. So she spoke with him about all that was in her heart.

9. And then she said, "I would have lost heart, unless I had believed that I would see the goodness of YAH-way in the land of the living. Now I have hope. Thank you for loving me."

10. Now in Shushan, before a girl's turn came to visit King Xerxes, she had to complete twelve months of beauty treatments: six months with oil of myrrh and six with massage and special diet, perfumes and cosmetics. Thus prepared, each young woman would go to the king. In the evening she would go there and the next morning return to the harem. She would not go to the king again unless he asked for her by name.

11. When it was Esther's turn to go to the king, she accepted the advice of Hegai, the eunuch in charge of the harem, dressing according to his instructions.

12. Now the king was attracted to Esther more than to any of the other women, and she won his favor and approval more than any of the other virgins. So he set a royal crown on her head and made her queen instead[36] of Vashti. And the king gave a great banquet for all his nobles and officials. He proclaimed a holiday throughout the provinces and distributed gifts with royal liberality.

+13. She continued to worship YAH-way without abandoning her Jewish ways, but one day she learned the details of a plot by a man named Haman, the prime minister, to kill every Jew in the whole Persian Empire.

14. Haman told the king, "There is a certain race of people scattered among the nations all over your empire. They observe customs that are not like those of any other people. Moreover, they do not obey the laws of the empire, so it is not in your best interests to tolerate them. If it pleases the king, let a

---

[36]*Xerxes*

15. decree be issued to destroy them. I will pay $20,000,000 into the royal treasury for the expenses involved."

15. The king took off his ring, which was used to stamp official proclamations, and gave it to Haman to seal the decree that was to be written against the Jews.[37]

16. The king told him, "Keep the money, but go ahead and do as you like with these people--whatever you think best."

17. In her quarters, Queen Esther prayed to the God of Israel, "Give me courage, King of all gods and Ruler over all earthly powers. I am all alone, and I have no one to turn to but you. All the king's officials and the people of the royal provinces want the whole world to praise worthless idols and stand in awe of mortal kings forever."

18. Then Esther said, "Anyone, whether man or woman, who goes into the king's inner court without his summons is doomed to die unless the king holds out his golden scepter; and the king has not called for me to come to him in more than a month. But I will go to the king, even though it is against the law. And if I perish, I perish."

19. She combined womanly emotion with manly courage.

20. Three days later Esther put on her royal robes and stood in the inner court of the palace, in front of the king's hall. The king was sitting on his royal throne in the hall, facing the entrance. Queen Esther's face[38] was radiantly beautiful. She looked as cheerful as she was lovely, but in her heart she was terror-stricken. She grew weak and turned pale; she almost fainted and had to lean her head on her attendant's shoulder.

21. "What is it, Esther?" he said to her. "I am your

---

[37] *Liberality*
[38] *Scepter*

husband. There's no need to be afraid. You will not die. Come here to me."

22. He lifted his gold scepter and touched her on the neck with it.

23. Then he kissed her and said, "Tell me what you want."

24. So she spoke with him about all that was in her heart.

25. "If it pleases the king," she said, "and if he regards me with favor and thinks it the right thing to do, and if he is pleased with me, grant me my life--this is my petition. And spare my people--this is my request. Let an order be written overruling the dispatches that Haman devised and wrote to destroy the Jews in all the king's provinces. For I am a Jew. We do not worship idols made of silver and gold--the work of men's hands. They have mouths, but they do not speak; eyes they[39] have, but they do not see; they have ears, but they do not hear; noses they have, but they do not smell; they have hands, but they do not handle; feet they have, but they do not walk; nor do they mutter through their throat. I have not been led astray to honor them by kissing my hand in reverence to them."

+26. Then Queen Esther said, "We are not traitors at all but are governed by very just laws. We worship the living YAH-way, the highest and greatest God, who dwells in our inmost heart and helps us to understand what is good and wise when we listen quietly and humbly. Have I ever failed to please you, or has my faith in this God ever stopped me from performing my duties as queen?"

27. Later that same day King Xerxes agreed to overturn his decree, and he said, "I thought it best to begin making plans for the general welfare of the

---

[39] *Petition*

people."[40]

Eight--Kelli

+1. At this same time, in the land of Cherokee and Plymouth, there was a song in the wind and it was saying, "Do what seems best to you. Rest and be at ease. Wear fine clothes and live happily. Eat, O friends! Drink, yes, drink deeply, O beloved ones! No one is compelled to drink, but each should do according to his pleasure. Wine gladdens the heart of man, oil makes his hair shine, and bread sustains his heart. Go, eat your bread with joy and drink your wine with a very merry spirit."

+2. The name of one young woman in this land was Kelli, and she was lovely and beautiful. Many who saw her gained a feeling of pleasure.

+3. One day she asked herself, "Whom should I serve?"

+4. Before long, a man appeared in front of her eyes. His name was Mike, and he said within him, "I will allure her, and speak to her heart with words of romance."

+5. Their paths crossed at times and they slowly formed a tenuous bond of trust and anticipation.[41]

+6. On one occasion, they happened by chance to meet in darkness near her home, and Mike spoke to her in a delightful way.

+7. "See, the winter is past, the rains are over and gone. The flowers appear on the earth; the time of singing

---
[40]*Throat*
[41]*Cherokee*

	has come, and the song of doves is heard in the fields. The apple tree puts forth her green apples, and the vines with the tender grapes give a good smell. Join me, my doe, my fair one, and come away!"
+8.	"Like a lily among thorns, so is my darling among the daughters. O my dove, all alone in secret places, let me see and hear your face and voice; for your voice is sweet and your countenance is exquisite."
+9.	"You inflame me, my sister, my spouse, because of your youthful breasts. Better than wine is your erotic charm, and better than all spices is the scent of your perfumes."
+10.	"You whom I desire are as beautiful as Tirzah, as captivating as Jerusalem, awesome as an army with banners! Turn your eyes away from me, for they have overwhelmed me."[42]
+11.	Then Kelli's mother stepped outside, and asked, "Is everything all right? Why did this madman come, and what does he want with you?"
+12.	She answered, "You know why. He came for beauty. Leave him alone. We're fine."
+13.	When her mother went back into the house, Kelli said, "Behold, you are handsome, my stallion! Yes, pleasant! Your lips, my partner, drip as the honeycomb. Honey and milk are under your tongue, and the fragrance of your garments is like the fragrance of Lebanon: of saffron and cinnamon, and incense of every kind, myrrh and aloes, with all the most fragrant perfumes. You are a fountain of gardens, a well of living waters. Please do not deceive me. Now I am going."
14.	Then she left and walked through the door of her home.

---

[42] *Breasts*

+15. The next eve, she put paint on her eyes and adorned her head, and looked through a window, hoping.

+16. In her heart she said, "I am dark, but sexy, because the sun has[43] tanned me. He is like a gazelle or a young stag. Does he stand behind our wall, looking through the windows, gazing through the lattice? Take me away with you--hurry! One of my town's leaders has brought me into his chambers. I wish it would happen never again."

+17. As the hour grew late, she lay down for a nap. Then a knock awoke her.

+18. My favorite spoke, and said to me: "Rise up, my doe, my fair one, and come away. Open your mouth wide, and I will fill it."

19. "I have taken off my dress, how can I put it on again? I have washed my feet, how can I dirty them again?"

+20. I heard my amatory fellow put his hand by the latch of the door, and my heart yearned for him. I arose to open the handles of the lock.

+21. But my desirable one had turned away and was gone. And my heart was wounded within me.[44]

+22. By night on my bed, I sought the one I desired; I sought him but did not find him.

23. I sleep, but my heart is awake. I hear his voice! He knocks, saying, "Open for me, my sister, my friend, my dove, my perfect one." I said to him, "Did not my heart go with you when you left?"

+24. Let him kiss me with his mouth. You make me feel better

---

[43] *Stallion*
[44] *Wounded*

than wine can. Because of your fragrance, your name pours forth like oil, and the virgins desire you.

+25. The next morning she said, "I bid you, O daughters of my village, if you find my sexy stallion, that you tell him I am pining away! The heart knows its own bitterness, and a stranger does not share its joy."

+26. "What is your stallion more than another, O fairest among women? How is he different from any other, that we should give you our promise?"

+27. Kelli replied, "My boyfriend is white and ruddy, distinguished among ten[45] thousand. His head is like the finest gold. His curls are wavy, and black as a raven. His eyes are like doves by the water streams, washed in milk, mounted like jewels. His cheeks are like a bed of spices, like banks of scented herbs. His lips are lilies, dripping liquid myrrh. His hands are rods of gold set with beryl. His body is carved ivory inlaid with sapphires. His thighs are columns of alabaster set in sockets of gold. He is majestic, like the Lebanon Mountains with their towering cedars. His mouth is altogether sweet. Everything about him enchants me. This is my man and this is my friend, O daughters of my town!"

28. The other girls answered, "Very well. A man is valued by what others say of him, and you have convinced us."

29. "What a blessing this has been to me. My perfume goes forth like a cluster of henna blossoms, while my man is resting all night upon my breasts."

+30. "I am my wooer's and his desire is toward me. My darling is mine, and I am his. I feel his left hand under my head, and his right hand embraces me. He brings me to the banqueting house and his

---

[45]*Distinguished*

banner over me is[46] full of adoration."

+31. "Where has your amative companion gone, O fairest among women? Where has he turned aside, that we may seek him with you?"

32. "There he is: the voice of my man! Behold, he comes leaping upon the mountains, skipping upon the hills."

33. He says, "Who is she who looks forth as the morning, fair as the moon, clear as the sun? How fair and how pleasant you are, O lady, with your delights!"

34. "Then tell me, that I may know--for surely you would not deceive with your lips."

+35. "I have compared you, sexy one, to my filly among Pharaoh's chariots. Your cheeks are erotic with ornaments, your neck with chains of gold. Behold, you are fair, my companion! You have dove's eyes behind your veil. Your hair is like a flock of goats going down from Mount Gilead. Your teeth are like a flock of shorn sheep which have come up[47] from the washing, every one of which bears twins, and none is barren among them. Your lips are like a strand of scarlet, and your mouth is lovely. Your temples are like a piece of pomegranate. Your two breasts are like two fawns, twins of a gazelle, which feed among the lilies."

36. "You have ravished my heart, my sister, my spouse, with one look of your eyes, with one link of your necklace."

+37. She says, "Tell me, O you whom I want, where you work in the day, where you make your flock rest at noon."

---

[46] *Ivory*
[47] *Skipping*

38.	"If you do not know, O fairest among women, follow in the footsteps of the flock."
+39.	Kelli dismisses: "Until the day breaks and the shadows flee away, turn, my sexy one, and be like a gazelle or a young stag on the mountains of Separation."
+40.	And Mike departs: "Until the day breaks and the shadows flee away,[48] I will go my way to the mountain of myrrh and to the hill of frankincense."
+41.	Three days passed. During the night I saw him again in a dream.
+42.	"I will rise now," I said, "and go about the city streets and seek the one I long for."
+43.	I asked the watchmen of the city, "Have you seen the one that I want?"
+44.	Scarcely had I passed them by, when I found the one I wanted. I held him and would not let him go, until I brought him to my mother's house.
45.	"Let my life now be precious in your sight. My breasts are like towers, the desire of your eyes."
+46.	"Sustain me with raisin cakes, refresh me with apples, for I am smitten to the heart. Come, king Eros, let us go forth to the field; let us lodge in the villages. Set me as a seal upon your heart and arm. For passion is as strong as death, jealousy as cruel as the grave. Its flames are[49] flames of fire, a blazing flame, nor can the floods drown it."
+47.	"Awake, north wind, and come, O south, blow upon my garden, that its spices may flow out. Let my

---

[48] *Ravished*
[49] *Smitten*

	lusty gallant come to his garden and eat its pleasant fruits."
48.	He told me, "Behold, you are fair, my friend. You have dove's eyes. How beautiful are your feet in sandals, the curves of your thighs are like jewels."
+49.	"Your navel is a rounded goblet, your waist is a heap of wheat tied in a string."
50.	"Your neck is like an ivory tower, your eyes like the pools in Heshbon. Your nose is perfect beauty. You are tall and slim like a palm tree, and your breasts like its clusters. I will go up to the palm tree, I will take hold of its branches. Let now your breasts be like clusters of the vine, the fragrance of your breath like apples, and the roof of your mouth like the best wine."[50]

+51. "I must give her all she desires, whatever she asks," is in his thoughts.

+52. Meanwhile she decides, "I will bow down upon my knees. Yes, I will drink and swallow. Like an apple tree in the woods, his fruit shall be sweet to my taste."

+53. Then Kelli speaks with rapid pulse, "Make haste, my erotically-charged honeybuns. Be like a gazelle or a young stag on the mountains of spices. Let us get up early to the vineyards. Let us see if the vine has budded, whether the grape blossoms are open, and the pomegranates are in bloom. There I will let you go into me, for you are greatly beloved."

+54. Soon thereafter, Mike went into his favorite daughter in all the land.

---

[50]*Thighs*

Nine--Onias

+1. Year by year this spirit became an overpowering presence in the[51] region, and to the ends of the earth.

2. It said, "I am it and there is none besides me."

+3. Because of the multitude of spiritual unfaithfulness, and the temptations of the seductive harlot, the people, whether small or great, whether man or woman, were led to believe.

4. But thus says the Holy One of Israel, the God of the Hebrews, the everlasting King: "Wine, women, and song have robbed my people of their brains. How long will you refuse to humble yourself before Me?"

+5. There was one man, named Onias, the former High Priest in Jerusalem, who had shown wisdom and maintained self-control throughout his whole life. He was a great and wonderful man of humble and gentle disposition, who was an outstanding orator and who had been taught from childhood how to live a virtuous life.

6. "As for me, I have not hurried away from being a shepherd who follows You. You are fairer than the sons of men; grace is poured upon Your[52] lips."

7. "Woe to the foolish prophets, who follow their own spirit."

8. "Look, all you who kindle a fire, who encircle yourselves with sparks. Walk in the light of your fire and in the sparks you have kindled. This you shall have from My hand: you shall lie down in torment."

9. "Woe to her who is rebellious and polluted."

10. "You are trusting in the staff of this broken reed, on

---
[51] *Honeybuns*
[52] *Robbed*

	which if a man leans, it will pierce his hand."
11.	"For your faithfulness is like a morning cloud, and like the early dew it goes away."
12.	"Roll yourself in the dust. Pass by in naked shame, you inhabitant of Beautiful."
+13.	He mourned and was moved to tears when he saw the people's[53] waywardness.
14.	"What have you done? Listen while I sing you this song, a song of my Friend and his vineyard. My Friend had a vineyard on a very fertile hill."
15.	My Friend says, "Is there anything I failed to do for it? Then why did it produce sour grapes and not the good grapes I expected?"
16.	"For the men of Judah are His pleasant plant. He looked for justice, but behold, oppression; for righteousness, but behold, there was wailing and weeping. You are filled with shame instead of glory."
+17.	"You call for your lovers, but they will deceive you. Why do you commit this great evil against yourselves?"
+18.	Then Onias spoke to all the house of Israel, saying, "If you return to the YAH-way with all your hearts, and put away the foreign gods and images of Canaanite goddesses from among you, and prepare your hearts to serve YAH-way alone, then the Spirit of the YAH-way will come upon you, and you will be turned into a different person."[54]

---

[53] *Kindle*
[54] *Waywardness*

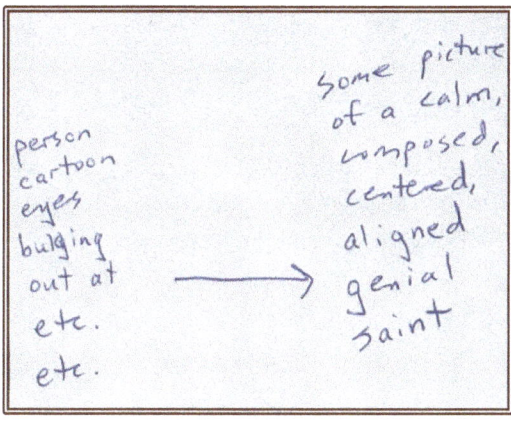

19. "Come back to the YAH-way quickly. Don't think that you can keep putting it off."

20. "All flesh is grass, and all its loveliness is like the flower of the field. The grass withers because the breath of YAH-way blows upon it. Surely the people are grass. The flower fades, but the word of our God stands forever."

21. "In the way of righteousness is life, and in its pathway there is no death!"

+22. "Without obedience to the YAH-way's great goodness, life becomes only sad, sad news for everyone."

23. "The land has committed great spiritual adultery by departing from the YAH-way. For the spirit of harlotry has caused them to stray, and they have played the whore against their God."

+24. "She adorned herself with her earrings and jewelry, and went after her lovers."[55]

25. "And you washed yourself for them, painted your eyes, and decorated yourselves with ornaments. People of Israel, all over the land you have sold

---

[55] Lovers

yourselves like prostitutes; you have loved for reward on every threshing floor."

+26. "Holding and touching is not a sin, but you have gone too far! You think intercourse has no purpose but pleasure. Bethink yourselves! I have made the world like a womb, so that it produces new human beings at regular intervals. Intercourse is the continuation of physical life. Trying to circumvent this design harms everything."

27. "Because you have forgotten Me and trusted in falsehood, therefore you shall stumble in the day."

28. "And when you are plundered, what will you do? Though you clothe yourself with crimson, though you adorn yourself with ornaments of gold, though you enlarge your eyes with paint, in vain you will make yourself fair; your lovers will despise you and want to kill you."

29. "Run to and fro through the streets of Jerusalem. If you can find[56] one person who does justice, who seeks truth, then I will pardon the whole land."

30. "For My eyes are on all their ways; they are not hidden from My face, nor is their iniquity hidden from Me."

31. Then YAH-way spoke to Onias and said, "Give your love to a woman who is committing adultery, even as YAH-way loves the children of Israel, though they turn to other gods and love the raisin cakes of the pagans."

+32. "Nevertheless My lovingkindness I will not utterly take from them, nor allow My faithfulness to fail."

33. "And I will make an everlasting covenant with them, that I will not turn away from doing them good; but I will put My fear in their hearts so that they will not

---

[56] *Bethink*

depart from Me."[57]

---

[57] *Everlasting*

Piety (Pi)

One--Simon

1. In the first year of Simon, high priest, governor, and leader of the Jews, Simon heard these words from the YAH-way, for he was a faithful man and feared God more than many.

+2. "Why do you beautify your appearance to seek the love of women? Therefore you have also taught them your deceptive ways. And your sins have withheld good things from you. For among My people are found wicked men. They lie in wait as one who sets snares. They set traps to catch men and women. As a cage is full of birds, so are their houses full of deceit. Thus they have become great and grown rich. They have done disgraceful things in Israel. Indeed I know, and am a witness. In accordance with the wisdom which is in your possession, instruct those who do not know My laws."

+3. "Yes, YAH-way, I will obey your voice, for You are my Father."

4. Then I proclaimed a fast on the bank of the Jordan River, that we might humble ourselves before our God, to seek the right way for us and our little ones, and all our possessions, in all matters concerning[1] the people, for the common good, both in their private and public lives.

+5. And Simon says, "If a man entices and lies with a virgin who is not engaged, he must pay the bride price for her and marry her. But if she refuses to marry him, he must still pay her father a sum of money equal to the bride price for a virgin girl."

+6. "If a man finds a girl who is a virgin, who is not

---
[1] *Simon*

engaged, and seizes her and rapes her and they are discovered, then the man who lay with her shall give to the girl's father fifty shekels of silver, and, if she agrees, she shall become his wife because he has violated her. He cannot divorce her all his days."

7. "If you lend money to any Jews who are poor among you, you shall not charge interest."

8. "You shall not circulate a false report, and do not help a guilty man by giving false testimony."

9. "You shall not show partiality nor pervert the judgment of a poor man[2] in his dispute."

10. "Do not kill the innocent or the righteous."

11. "If anyone sins by refusing to return a deposit on something borrowed or rented, or by refusing to return something entrusted to him, or by robbery, or by oppressing his neighbor, or by finding a lost article and lying about it, swearing that he doesn't have it--on the day he is found guilty of any such sin, he shall restore what he took, adding a twenty percent fine, and give it to the one he has harmed."

+12. "If any man has an emission of semen, then he shall wash all his body in water. And any garment and any leather on which there is semen, it shall be washed with water. Also, when a woman lies with a man, and there is an emission of semen, they both shall bathe in water. After the night is over, they are cleansed and restored to a sanitary state."

13. "You shall not do as they do in the land of Egypt, where you once lived, nor shall you do as they do in the land of Canaan; do not conform to their customs. You must obey my laws and be careful to follow my[3] decrees. You will save your life by doing so."

---

[2] *Entices*
[3] *Semen*

+14. Simon further continued his speaking, and said: "If you diligently heed the voice of the YAH-way your God and do what is commanded, then your diseases shall be few, for the YAH-way is the God who heals you."

15. "If you do well, will you not be accepted? And if you do not do well, sin is crouching at your door. It wants to rule you, but you must overcome it."

16. "None of you shall approach any blood relative of his flesh to uncover nakedness. You shall not uncover the nakedness of your mother. You shall not uncover the nakedness of your father's wife."

17. "The nakedness of your sister, the daughter of your father, or the daughter of your mother, whether born at home or elsewhere, their nakedness you shall not uncover."

18. "The nakedness of your son's daughter or your daughter's daughter,[4] their nakedness you shall not uncover. You shall not uncover the nakedness of your father's sister; she is your father's blood relative. You shall not uncover the nakedness of your mother's sister, for she is your mother's blood relative."

+19. "You shall not uncover the nakedness of your father's brother's wife; she is your aunt. You shall not uncover the nakedness of your daughter-in-law; she is your son's wife; you shall not have intercourse with her."

20. "You shall not uncover the nakedness of your brother's wife."

21. "You shall not have intercourse with a woman and

---

[4]*Diseases*

	also with her daughter. Do not have sexual relations with either her son's daughter or her daughter's daughter; they are her close relatives."
22.	"Do not take your wife's sister and have sexual relations with her."
+23.	"Also there must be no sexual activity with a woman during the time of her menses."[5]
24.	"And you shall not have intercourse with your neighbor's wife."
+25.	"A man shall not have anal or oral intercourse with another man."
26.	"Also you shall not have intercourse with any animal, nor shall any woman set herself in front of a beast to mate with it; such things are abhorrent."
27.	"Do not turn to idols, nor make for yourselves molded gods."
28.	"You shall not steal, nor deal falsely. Do not deceive one another."
29.	"Never oppress a poor hired man, whether he is a fellow Israelite or a foreigner living in one of your towns. The wages of a hired servant shall not remain with you all night until the morning. You shall give him his pay on the day he earns it, before the sun goes down; for he is poor, and sets his heart upon it. Otherwise he may cry out to the YAH-way against you and it would be counted as a sin in you."
+30.	"Honor God in this way, and you will receive a good reward."[6]
31.	"Keep a close watch on yourself, in everything you

---

[5] *Aunt*
[6] *Animal*

do, and discipline yourself in all your conduct."

32. "Do to no one what you yourself dislike. Never do to anyone else anything that you would not want someone to do to you."

33. "You shall not bear hatred for your brother in your heart. You shall not go about spreading gossip and scandal among your people. When someone is on trial for his life, speak out if your testimony can help him."

34. "You shall not cut yourselves nor put tattoo marks upon your body."

35. "Do not degrade your daughter by making her a prostitute, lest the land fall into harlotry and become full of wickedness."

36. "Do not go for advice to people who consult the spirits of the dead. Do not seek out wizards, to be defiled by them."

37. "Fear God, and give due honor and respect to the elderly."[7]

---

[7] *Dislike*

38.	"Use honest scales when measuring length, weight or quantity. Do not cheat anyone."
+39.	"Your God is not pleased with having anything less than your whole heart. He punishes a father's iniquity to the third or fourth generation of the father's children, but shows mercy to a thousand generations of those who love and keep the YAH-way's commandments."
+40.	"A priest should never defile himself by touching a dead person. A priest shall not marry a woman who has been a prostitute, nor a woman who has been divorced by her husband; for the priest is holy. And he who is the high priest shall take a virgin of his own people as wife."
41.	"When you reap the harvest of your land, do not reap to the very edges of your field. You shall leave them for poor people and foreigners. When you reap your harvest in your field, and forget a sheaf in the field, you shall not go back to get it; it shall be for the stranger, the fatherless, and the widow, that the YAH-way may bless[8] you in all the work of your hands."
42.	"When you beat your olive trees, you shall not go over the boughs again. When you have gathered your grapes once, do not go back over the vines a second time. And you shall remember that you were a slave in the land of Egypt; therefore, I command you to do this thing."
+43.	"You shall have the same law for the stranger and the native of your land."
44.	"Seven weeks of years shall you count--seven times seven years--so that the seven cycles amount to forty-nine years. Then, on the tenth day of the

---

[8]*Quantity*

seventh month let the trumpet resound; on this, the Day of Atonement, the trumpet blast shall re-echo throughout your land. This fiftieth year you shall make sacred by proclaiming liberty in the land for all its inhabitants. It shall be a jubilee for you, when every one of you shall return to his own property, every one to his own family estate. In this fiftieth year, you shall not plant your fields or harvest the grain that grows by itself or gather the grapes in your unpruned vineyards."[9]

45. "Therefore, when you sell any land to your neighbor or buy any from him, do not deal unfairly. On the basis of the number of years since the last jubilee shall you purchase the land from him; and so also, on the basis of the number of years for crops, shall he sell it to you. When the years are many, the price shall be so much the more; when the years are few, the price shall be so much the less. For it is really the number of crops that he sells you."

46. "You shall not mistreat one another, but you shall fear your God."

47. "Six years you shall sow your field, and six years you shall prune your vineyard, and gather in its fruit. But in the seventh year there shall be a sabbath of solemn rest for the land, a sabbath to YAH-way. You shall neither sow your field nor prune your vineyard. What grows of its own accord of your harvest you shall not reap, nor gather the grapes of your untended vine, for it is a year of rest for the land."

48. "Follow my decrees and be careful to obey my laws, and you will live safely in the land. The land will yield its fruit and you will have food in abundance, so that you may live there without worry. Therefore, do[10] not say, 'What shall we eat in the seventh year, if

---

[9]*Estate*
[10]*Jubilee*

	we do not then sow or reap our crop?'"
+49.	"For you will be blessed in the sixth year so that the land will produce enough food for two years. When you plant your fields in the eighth year, you will still be eating what you harvested during the sixth year, and you will have enough to eat until the crops you plant that year are harvested."
50.	"If a fellow Israelite living near you becomes poor and cannot support himself, you must provide for him as you would for a hired man, so that he can continue to live near you. Do not charge him any interest on the money you lend him, and do not make a profit on the food you sell him, but obey God."
51.	"And if your brother becomes poor beside you, and sells himself to you, you shall not make him serve as a slave: he shall be with you as a hired servant and as a sojourner. He shall serve with you until the year of the jubilee. You shall not rule over him with harshness."[11]
52.	"Remember all the commandments of the YAH-way, so as to do them and not follow after the desires of your own heart and your own eyes, and be holy to your God."
+53.	"When your children ask you, 'What is the purpose of these laws?' then you shall say, 'YAH-way commands us always to observe these for our good and for our preservation.'"
54.	"When you have eaten and are full, then you shall bless the YAH-way."
55.	"Beware that you never forget your God by not obeying the commandments of the YAH-way,

---

[11] *Sojourner*

lest--when you have eaten and are satisfied, and have built beautiful houses and dwell in them, and when your herds and your flocks multiply, and your silver and your gold are increased, and all that you have is multiplied--then you say in your heart, 'My own power and strength has gained me all this.'"

56. "At the end of every third year you shall bring out all the tithes of your produce for that year, that the Levite, and also the alien, the orphan and the widow who belong to your community may come and eat and[12] be satisfied, that the YAH-way may bless you in all the work of your hand which you do."

57. "If you see your brother's donkey or his ox fallen on the road, do not ignore it. You shall surely help him to lift them up again."

58. "A woman shall not wear anything that pertains to a man, nor shall a man put on a woman's garment. It is lewdness."

59. "When a man has taken a new wife, he shall not go out to war or be drafted into any other public duty. He shall be free at home for one year to give happiness to his wife."

60. "You will no longer go your own way as you do now, everyone doing whatever he thinks is right. These are the statutes and judgments which you shall be careful to observe all the days that you live on the earth."

+61. Simon says, "Stop your loud boasting; silence your proud words. For YAH-way is the God of knowledge, who knows and weighs all our[13] actions."

62. "You shall not fear other gods, nor bow down to

---

[12] *Purpose*
[13] *Lewdness*

them nor serve them nor sacrifice to them."

63. "Oh, fear the YAH-way, you his saints! Those who fear him lack nothing."

+64. "No good thing will be withheld from those who seek the YAH-way and who walk uprightly with honesty."

65. "Watch the blameless man, and observe the upright; for the future of that man is peace."

+66. "Listen to the words of the YAH-way."

67. "When you eat the labor of your hands, you shall be happy, and it shall be well with you. Your wife shall be like a fruitful vine in the very heart of your house, your children like olive plants all around your table."[14]

68. Then he said to the judges, "Take heed to what you are doing, for you do not judge for man but for YAH-way, who is with you in the judgment. Now therefore, let the fear of the YAH-way be upon you. Take care and do it, for there is no iniquity with the YAH-way our God, no partiality, nor taking of bribes."

69. "For YAH-way loves the righteous. Thus you shall act with a loyal heart. Do this, and you will not be guilty."

+70. "Also it shall not be lawful to impose a tax on any of the priests, Levites, singers, gatekeepers, or servants of the house of God."

71. "Walk in God's Law. Observe and do all the commandments of the YAH-way our Lord."

---

[14] *Labor*

Two

+1. Simon says, "Each man should be master in his own house. Every[15] woman should treat her husband with proper respect, whether he is rich or poor."

2. "YAH-way hates cheating and delights in honesty."

3. "Do not rob the poor."

4. "When dining with a rich man, do not desire his delicacies, for they are deceptive food."

5. "Do not eat the bread of a man who is stingy, for he is like one who is inwardly reckoning. 'Eat and drink!' he says to you, but his heart is not with you."

6. "Do not go hastily to court. For what will you do in the end, when your neighbor has put you to shame? Discuss the matter with him privately. Don't tell anyone else, lest he who hears it expose your shame, and your reputation be ruined."

7. "Better is a neighbor nearby than a brother far away."[16]

8. "Be diligent to know the state of your flocks, and attend to your herds, for riches can disappear fast. When the hay is removed, and the tender grass shows itself, and the herbs of the mountains are gathered in, the lambs will provide your clothing, and the goats the price of a field. You shall have enough goats' milk for your food, for the food of your household, and the nourishment of your maidservants."

---

[15] *Impose*
[16] *Reputation*

9.	"Obey the king. Those who obey him will experience nothing harmful."
10.	"Feast at the proper time--for strength and not for drunkenness!"
11.	"In the morning sow your seed, and in the evening do not withhold your hand. For you do not know which will prosper, either this or that, or whether both alike will be good. Take heed now that you do not fail to do this."
12.	"It will go well with the righteous, for they will eat the fruit of their actions. Woe to the wicked! It will go badly with him, for what he deserves will be done to him."[17]
+13.	"He who walks righteously and speaks truthfully, who despises the gain of fraud and of oppressions, who shakes his hand free from the taking of bribes, his bread will be given to him and his water will be in sure supply."
14.	"Who among you fears the YAH-way? Who obeys the voice of His servant? Who walks in darkness and has no light? Let him trust in the name of YAH-way and rely upon his God."
15.	"Preserve justice, and do righteousness. How blessed is the man who does this, and the son of man who takes hold of it; who keeps from profaning the sabbath, and keeps his hand from doing any evil."
+16.	"If you turn your foot from doing pleasure on the holy day, and call the sabbath a delight, and honor the YAH-way, not doing your own ways, nor finding your own pleasure, nor speaking your own words, and keep the words of this covenant, and do them,

---

[17]*Nourishment*

	then you will prosper in all that you do."
+17.	"With God's help, may we never abandon the Law or disobey these commands."[18]
18.	"It is right that all mortals should be subject to God and not think that they are his equal."
19.	"He who hears, let him hear, and he who refuses, let him refuse."
20.	"No one will strengthen himself who lives in iniquity."
21.	"Do not rejoice with joy like other peoples, for they do not know to do right who store up violence and robbery in their mansions."
22.	"You shall no more worship the work of your hands, and do not prattle, but be silent in the presence of the Lord YAH-way."
23.	"Be strong, all you people of the land, and work."
+24.	"Turn now from your self-minded ways and deeds. Then all nations will call you blessed, for you will live in a delightful land."
25.	"Every day of your life, keep the YAH-way in mind. Never sin deliberately or disobey any of his commands. Always do what is right[19] and never get involved in anything evil. Be honest, and you will succeed in whatever you do."
26.	"Give generously. If you are stingy in giving to the poor, God will be stingy in giving to you. Give according to what you have. The more you have, the more you should give. Even if you have only a little, be sure to give something."

---

[18]*Fraud*
[19]*Mansions*

27.	"The wife of your youth is your companion, and your wife by covenant. But did the YAH-way not make one of you both? And why one? For godly offspring. Therefore take heed to your spirit, and let none deal treacherously with the wife of his youth."
28.	"When you are about to have intercourse with her, both of you first rise up to pray."
29.	"Be on your guard against prostitutes."
30.	"Do not drink so much wine that you get drunk, and do not let drinking become a habit."[20]
31.	"Give food to the hungry and clothes to people in need. If you are prosperous, give generously, and do it gladly!"
32.	"If you obey God and avoid sin, the YAH-way will be pleased and make you prosperous. It is better to pray sincerely and to please God by helping the poor than to be rich and dishonest. It is better to give to the poor than to store up gold."
33.	"Praise the everlasting God by doing what he demands. Worship God sincerely. Bring up your children to do what is right. Teach them that they must give to the poor and be mindful of God at all times."
+34.	"If a man should walk in a false spirit and speak a lie, saying, 'I will trust in futile things!' he deceives himself, and futility will be his reward."
+35.	"To fear the YAH-way is the flower of Prudence that blossoms with peace and good health."
36.	"Be faithful in the practice of your religion. When

---

[20] *Drunk*

you worship[21] YAH-way, do it with all your heart."

37. "Be careful about what you say, and don't be a hypocrite. Don't be arrogant; you may suffer a fall and be disgraced."

38. "If you are going to serve YAH-way, be prepared for times when you will be put to the test. Be sincere and determined. Keep calm when trouble comes."

+39. "Compassionate and merciful is the YAH-way, by forgiving our sins and keeping us safe in time of trouble."

40. "Never seek honor for yourself at your father's expense; it is not to your credit if he is dishonored."

41. "Even to the death fight for truth, and the YAH-way your God will battle for you."

42. "Don't be quick to speak or lazy and negligent in your work. Don't act like a lion at home or be suspicious of your servants. Don't stick out[22] your hand to get something if you're going to be tightfisted when the time comes to pay it back."

43. "Don't think that you can sin and get away with it. Don't be so certain of YAH-way's forgiveness that you go on committing one sin after another."

44. "If you are polite and courteous, you will enjoy the friendship of many people."

45. "Don't think up lies to tell about your friends. Don't tell lies at all. It never does any good."

46. "Don't look too intently at a virgin, or you may find yourself forced to pay a bride price."

---

[21] *Mindful*
[22] *Suspicious*

47. "No matter the wrong, do no violence to your neighbor. Don't be angry with someone for every little thing. Don't do anything out of injured pride."[23]

48. "Stand by your duty and stick to it. Grow old at your work."

49. "No good ever comes to a person who makes evil a habit or refuses to give to the poor."

50. "If you touch tar, it will stick to you, and if you keep company with arrogant people, you will come to be just like them."

51. "There is nothing wrong with being rich if you haven't sinned to get that way. But there is nothing sinful about being poor, either. Only the ungodly think so. It's what is in your heart that makes the expression on your face happy or sad."

52. "Return to the YAH-way, and leave your sin behind. Pray sincerely that he will help you live a better life. Turn again to the Most High and away from sin."

53. "Don't indulge in luxurious living; the expense of it will ruin you."

54. "Have you heard a rumor? Let it die with you. Be brave! It won't[24] make you explode."

55. "Don't fall into the habit of coarse, profane talk; it is sinful."

56. "No sufferings are worse than the sufferings caused by people who hate you. No revenge is worse than revenge taken by an enemy."

57. "If you don't pay attention to small matters, you will

---

[23] *Courteous*
[24] *Expression*

	gradually ruin yourself."
58.	"Never lose your head over a woman's beauty, and don't try to win a woman because she is wealthy. When a man is supported by his wife, there is sure to be anger, arrogance, and humiliation."
59.	"A bad wife is like a yoke that doesn't fit. Trying to control her is like holding a scorpion."
60.	"A daughter is a treasure that keeps her father awake at night, worrying about her. If she is young, he worries that she might not get married. If she is already married, he worries about her happiness."[25]
+61.	"If your daughter is determined to have her own way, keep a close watch on her. If you don't, she'll take advantage of any chance she gets, and she may make a fool of you in front of your enemies. Don't be too surprised if she disappoints you. She'll spread her legs anywhere for any man who wants her. She'll open her quiver for every arrow."
62.	"A lawless man will get a godless wife, as he deserves, but a man who honors the YAH-way will have a devout wife. A shameless wife enjoys making a disgrace of herself, but a modest wife will act modestly even alone with her husband."
63.	"A self-willed woman is a bitch, but a woman with a sense of decency honors God. A wife who honors her husband will seem wise to everyone; but if she dishonors him by her overbearing attitude, everyone will know that she is ungodly."
64.	"Anger and a hot temper are horrible things, but sinners have both."
65.	"Be kind. If your neighbor needs something, lend it

---

[25] *Explode*

to him. And[26] when you are in debt, pay it back as soon as you can. If you meet your obligations, you will always be able to borrow what you need."

66. "Count among your treasures the fact that you give to the poor. It will save you from all kinds of trouble and will be a better defense against your enemies than the strongest shield or stoutest spear."

67. "The necessities of life are water, food, clothing, and a home where you can have privacy. It is better to be poor and live under your own crude roof than to enjoy lavish banquets in other people's homes. Be happy with what you have, even if it isn't very much, and don't get a reputation for living off other people."

68. "If you are dining with a great man, don't let your mouth hang open, and don't say, 'Look at all that food!' It is impolite to have a greedy eye. Nothing in creation is greedier than the eye. Remember that gluttony is evil. Recognize that your neighbor feels as you do. Toward what he eyes, do not put out a hand, nor reach when he does for the same dish. Be considerate of the other people at the table and treat them the way you want to be treated."[27]

69. "When you get your food, eat it like a human being. Don't smack and slurp; nobody can stand that. It's good manners to be the first to stop eating; stuffing yourself is offensive. If there are many people present, don't try to be the first to be served."

70. "A little bit is plenty for anyone with good manners. Besides, you won't be short of breath when you go to bed. People who eat too much get stomach aches and cannot sleep. If you don't overeat, you can get a good night's sleep and wake up early the next morning feeling fine. But if you do get a stomach

---
[26] Quiver
[27] Gluttony

ache from eating too much, go vomit and you will feel better."

71. "Never rebuke a person when you have both been drinking. Don't hurt his feelings while he is having a good time. It's not the time to criticize anyone, or to ask him to pay back a debt."

72. "Nothing that comes from bribery or injustice will last, but the effects of loyalty will remain forever. Wealth that has been obtained dishonestly is like a stream that runs full during a thunderstorm, tumbling rocks along as it flows, but then suddenly goes dry."[28]

73. "It is wise to lock things up if you cannot trust your wife or if too many people are around. Keep an accurate record of any deposits you make or of anything you give or receive."

74. "You must not let your sins weigh you down or control you. Those who are chained by their sins are doomed."

75. "All this is worthwhile advice, and if you follow it, everyone will approve of your behavior."

76. "Now therefore, make confession to the YAH-way, God of your fathers.
Separate yourselves from the peoples of the land, and do His will."

77. "Let it be done according to the law. Arise, for this matter is your responsibility. Be of good courage, and do it."

78. Then all the congregation answered and said with a loud voice, "Yes! As you have said, so we must do."

+79. So Simon said, "It was YAH-way's pleasure for his

---

[28] *Slurp*

righteousness' sake[29] to magnify these instructions and revelations to us and to make them great and glorious."

80. "Let each return to his house in peace."

81. And all the congregation said, "Amen!"

+82. So all the people went home and joyfully ate and drank and shared what they had with those who had nothing. They celebrated because they understood what had been taught to them, all who had separated themselves from the filth of the nations of the land in order to seek the YAH-way, God of Israel.

83. "Remember now, O YAH-way, how I have walked before You in truth and with a loyal heart, with a peaceful heart, with a whole heart, and have done what is good in Your sight. Remember me, O my God, for good!"

+84. The words of Simon are ended.[30]

85. The land of Judea was at peace as long as Simon lived. In that day the fair virgins and strong young men enjoyed their times together. During his entire reign, he used his position of power and influence to do what was good for his people, and they were always pleased with him as their ruler.

86. The Jews farmed their land in peace; the land produced its crops and the trees bore fruit. The young men showed off their splendid military uniforms, while the old men sat around the city squares and talked about the great things that had happened. Simon supplied the cities with food and provided them with weapons of defense. His fame spread everywhere. He brought peace to the country, and Israel's joy knew no bounds.

87. Everyone lived in peace among his own grapevines and fig

---

[29]*Congregation*
[30]*Revelations*

trees, and no one made them afraid. In those days all the enemy kings had been defeated, and there was no one left in the land to fight the Jews. Simon provided help for all the poor among his people, and he suppressed all who were wicked and lawless.[31]

Three--Ezra

1. Now there was a day when the sons of God came to present themselves before the YAH-way, and Satan (the adversary and accuser) also came among them.

+2. Satan eyed Ezra and said, "What will be this boy's rule of life, and his work?"

3. He was a wise son, endowed with discretion and understanding. And Ezra came to Jerusalem, prepared his heart to study the Law of YAH-way, and to do it, and to teach.

+4. Over the years, day by day, he put his inner meditations in writing.

+5. And it was written in the book: "If you have run with the footmen, and become weary, then how can you contend with horses? And if you are wearied in the land of peace, how will you do in the flooding of the Jordan?"

6. "My sorrow is continually before me. I have been afflicted and ready to[32] die from my youth up. Oh, that God would grant me the thing that I long for!"

7. "For affliction does not come from the dust, nor does trouble spring from the ground; yet man is

---

[31] *Influence*
[32] *Satan*

	born to trouble, as the sparks fly upward."
8.	"Teach me, and I will hold my tongue. Show me how I have erred."
9.	"If I am wicked, woe to me."
10.	"Whoever heard me spoke well of me, and those who saw me commended me, because I rescued the poor who cried for help, and the fatherless who had none to assist him. The man who was dying blessed me; I made the widow's heart sing. I put on righteousness as my clothing; justice was my robe and my turban. I was eyes to the blind and feet to the lame. I was a father to the needy."
11.	"If I have seen a wanderer without clothing, or a poor man without covering (but no sojourner had to lodge in the street, for I have opened my doors to the traveler). If I have made gold my hope, or if I have[33] rejoiced because my wealth was great--Oh, that the Almighty would answer me!"
+12.	"YAH-way loves righteousness, and Your countenance beholds the upright. God's way is perfect, a shield to all who trust in the YAH-way."
13.	"Far be it from You to slay the righteous with the wicked. Shall not the Judge of all the earth do right?"
14.	"Hear me when I call, O God of my righteousness."
15.	"YAH-way abhors the deceitful man."
+16.	"My God, my God, why have You forsaken me? Why is there no response to my groans?"
17.	"Teach me Your way, O YAH-way, and lead me in a smooth path."

---

[33]*Traveler*

18. "Be of good courage, and He shall strengthen your heart. For the angel[34] of YAH-way encamps all around those who fear Him."

19. "The transgression of the wicked: there is no fear of God. Render to them what they deserve. They have fallen, but we have risen and stand upright."

20. "The righteous shall inherit the land, and dwell in it. Nevertheless man does not endure. My age is as nothing before You; certainly every man at his best is a mere breath. Every man walks about like a shadow; surely they busy themselves in vain. He amasses riches for someone else to spend."

21. "You love righteousness and hate wickedness."

22. "Offer to God thanksgiving, for in death there is no remembrance of You; in the grave who will give You thanks? Adrift among the dead, whom You remember no more, shall the dead arise and praise You? Shall Your lovingkindness be declared in the grave, and Your righteousness in the land of forgetfulness? Not so. The dead do not praise the YAH-way."[35]

23. YAH-way tells me, "Be still, and know that I am God."

24. "I will declare Your name to my brethren; in the midst of the congregation I will praise You. Yes, I will sing aloud of Your mercy in the morning."

25. "A prayer to the God of my life: let not those who wait for You be ashamed because of me; let not those who seek You be confounded because of me, O God of Israel."

26. "Your way, O God, is in holiness. Establish the just;

---

[34]*Groans*
[35]*Transgression*

	spare the poor and needy."
27.	"Teach me Your way, O YAH-way; I will walk in Your truth. Give me singleness of heart to fear Your name."
28.	"Let all who make vows to the YAH-way surely pay them."
+29.	"When you turn to YAH-way and obey, (for the YAH-way is a merciful God), you will not be forsaken or destroyed."[36]
30.	"The righteous shall flourish like a palm tree, but I will not allow those who deceive to stay in my house; no hypocrite will remain in my presence."
31.	"Happiness comes to those who are fair to others and are always just and good."
32.	"God will bless those who revere the YAH-way, both the small and the great."
33.	"Oh, that my ways were directed to keep Your statutes! Then I would not be ashamed when I look into all Your commandments."
34.	"Give to Your servant a hearing heart, that I may discern between good and evil."
35.	"When anyone sins against his neighbor, and is forced to take an oath before Your altar, then hear in heaven, and act and judge Your servants, condemning the wicked, by bringing his way on his own head, and acquit the one who is innocent."[37]
36.	"May the YAH-way look on it, and repay!"
37.	"You rebuke the proud. Cursed are those who

---

[36] *Confounded*
[37] *Hearing*

	wander from Your commandments."
+38.	"My foot stands in an even place. Your hands have fashioned me; give me good deliberation, that I may learn Your precepts."
39.	"Your word is a lamp to guide me and a light for my path, to keep me from stumbling."
+40.	"Can it indeed be that God will ever dwell among men on the earth?"
+41.	"The entrance of Your words gives light; it gives resourcefulness to the simple."
42.	"Look upon me and be merciful to me, as is Your custom toward those who love Your name."
+43.	"For You have formed my inward spirit, You have covered me in my[38] mother's womb."
44.	"Let my prayer be set before You as incense, the lifting up of my hands as the evening sacrifice."
45.	"Answer me speedily, O YAH-way; my spirit fails! Do not hide Your face from me. Cause me to hear Your lovingkindness in the morning; cause me to know the way in which I should walk."
46.	"Teach me to do Your will, for You are my God. May Your good Spirit lead me in the land of uprightness."
47.	"If the ruler's temper rises against you, do not abandon your position; conciliation and calmness pacifies great offenses."
48.	"No one has power over the spirit to retain the spirit, and no one has power in the day of death. There is no discharge in that war."

---

[38] *Rebuke*

49.	"He who deals with a slack hand becomes poor, but the hand of the diligent makes one rich."[39]
+50.	"Proud men end in shame, but in humility is equitable judgment."
51.	"He who trusts in his riches will fall, but the righteous will flourish like foliage. Lying lips are an abomination to YAH-way, but those who deal truthfully are His delight. He who walks in his uprightness fears the YAH-way."
+52.	"The silver-haired head is a crown of glory, if it is found in the way of righteousness. Prudence and integrity are signs of the maturity that should come with old age."
+53.	"She who has a bountiful eye will be blessed, for she gives of her bread to the poor."
54.	"For lack of wood, the fire dies out; and when there is no talebearer, strife subsides."
+55.	"Give to the poor and you will never be in need. If you close your eyes to the poor, many people will curse you. The righteous care about justice for the poor, but the wicked do not perceive the importance of[40] such knowledge."
56.	"He who pampers his servant from childhood will have him as a son in the end."
57.	"I will wait and hope for the YAH-way, who is hiding from the house of Jacob. But the God who is holy shall be hallowed in righteousness, that all peoples of the earth may know Your name and fear You. In that day a man will look to his Maker and have respect for the Holy One, more than in all

---

[39]*Know*
[40]*Foliage*

	riches."
58.	"And there will be a tabernacle for shade in the daytime from the heat, for a place of refuge, and for a shelter from storm and rain."
59.	"You drew near on the day I called on You, and said, 'Do not fear!'"
+60.	"Your eyes are open to all the ways of people, to give everyone according to their ways and according to the fruit of their doings."
61.	"I am weary with weariness."[41]
62.	"Is it not from the mouth of the Most High that woe and well-being proceed? Why should a living man complain for the punishment of his sins?"
63.	"Do you seek great things for yourself? Do not seek them; for behold, I will bring adversity on all flesh," says the YAH-way. "But I will give your life to you as a prize in all places, wherever you go."
64.	"Who is a God like You, pardoning iniquity?"
65.	"Your eyes are too pure to look on evil; why then do you tolerate the treacherous? Why are you silent while the wicked devour those more righteous than themselves?"
66.	"Is it right for you to be angry?"
67.	I told the YAH-way, "Yes, it is right for me to be angry, even to death!"
68.	"Can two walk together, unless they are agreed?"[42]
69.	"Hallelujah!"

---

[41] *Storm*
[42] *Tolerate*

70. "The YAH-way is fair and does not show partiality, and is not prejudiced against the poor. When someone prays who has been wronged, YAH-way listens."

71. "Be merciful with those who are poor. Don't keep them waiting for your generosity. YAH-way has commanded us to help the poor; don't refuse them the help they need."

72. "The tears running down a widow's cheek cry out in accusation against the one who has caused her distress."

73. "Those who are alive can give thanks to YAH-way, but can anyone in the world of the dead sing praise to the Most High? A person who is alive and well can sing the YAH-way's praises, but the dead, who no longer exist, have no way to give him thanks."

Do cockroaches go to cockroach hell when they die or get smushed? Of course not.

As the Bible teaches us, when people die, they go to Sheol. (Sixty-five verses use this word.)

When Jesus (God) died on a cross with a penitent thief next to him, Jesus promised this other man: "Truly I tell you, today you will be with me in Paradise." To a man who is hanging on a cross with large nails drilled through parts of his body, will being dead feel like paradise? Of course.

---

74. "O death! how bitter the thought of you for the man at peace amid his possessions, for the man unruffled and always successful, who still can[43] enjoy life's pleasures. O death! how welcome your sentence to the weak man of failing strength, tottering and always rebuffed, with no more sight, with vanished hope."

75. "Do not be afraid of death's decree. Remember that it came to those before you and will come to those

---

[43] *Accusation*

after you. YAH-way has decreed it for every living creature. Who are you to object to what the Most High wishes? In the world of the dead no one will care whether you lived ten years, a hundred, or a thousand."

76. "Those who worried and schemed to make money, but who left no trace of their work behind, they have all disappeared and gone down to the world of the dead. Others have come along to take their place."

77. "O Israel, how great is the universe in which God dwells! How vast! There is no end to it; there is no way to measure how wide or how high it is. You divided the earth with rivers."

78. "No one has ever gone up into heaven to get Wisdom and bring her down out of the clouds. No one has sailed across the seas to find[44] Wisdom or bought her with precious gold. No one knows how to get to her or how to discover the path that leads to her."

79. "God traced out all the way of understanding, and has given her to Israel. Since then she has appeared on earth, and moved among men."

+80. "Those who have put their trust in God will come to understand the truth of the YAH-way, and the faithful shall abide in love. Grace and mercy are shown to the ones whom God has chosen."

+81. "By your Intelligence you made man to rule all creation, to govern the world with holiness and righteousness, to administer justice with integrity. I am your slave, as was my mother before me. I am only human. I am not strong, and my life will be short. I have little understanding of the Law or of how to apply it. Give me the Intuition that sits beside your throne; give me a place among your

---

[44]*Welcome*

children."

82. "People say to themselves, 'Our life is short and full of sorrow, and when its end comes, there is no escape. No one has ever been known to come back from the world of the dead. We were born by chance, and[45] after life is over, we will be as if we had never been born at all. Our breath is no more than a puff of smoke; our mind is nothing. When this is quenched, our body will crumble into ashes, and our breath will become part of the empty air. In time, no one will remember anything we ever did, and even our names will be forgotten. Our lives will pass away like the traces of clouds and vanish like fog in the heat of the sun. Our time on earth is like a passing shadow.'"

83. "The wicked say, 'Come on, then, let us enjoy the good things that are real, and live in this world the way we did when we were young and free of care. Let us have our fill of costly wine and perfumes; let no meadow be free from our wantonness. We'll oppress the poor. We'll call ourselves right if we are strong enough to get what we want. Righteous people are nothing but a nuisance, so let's look for chances to get rid of them. We'll be cruel to them, and torment them; then we'll find out how calm and reasonable they are!' That is how evil people think."

84. "The children of ungodly people will not leave large families; they are like plants trying to take root on rock, like withering reeds along a river[46] bank."

+85. "They make the bushel smaller and the shekel bigger, and love to cheat with dishonest scales."

86. "Wisdom is with You and knows Your actions; she was present when You made the world. She knows what is right and in accordance with Your

---

[45]*Intelligence*
[46]*Quenched*

commands. Send her from the holy heavens so that she may work at my side, and I may learn what pleases You. She knows and understands everything, and will guide me intelligently in what I do. Her glory will protect me. Thus my deeds will be acceptable, and I shall judge Your people justly."

87. "All creation uses its power to punish unrighteous people, but it becomes mild and kind to those who put their trust in you."

88. "How fortunate are the people who can live now and obey your commands!"[47]

Four--Elijah

+1. There was also a man in the land whose name was Elijah. He was blameless and upright and avoided evil. He was a great and honorable man.

2. "Blessed be God. Thank you for being so kind and true."

+3. And the LORD said to Satan, "Have you noticed my servant Elijah? There is no one on earth like him."

4. But one time when he was in affliction, he implored the LORD his God, and humbled himself greatly before the God of his fathers.

5. "Take my life away and free me from this world; let my body return to the earth. I am tormented by insults I don't deserve, and weighed down with despair. YAH-way, don't reject my prayer."

6. As he was going up the road, some youths came from the

---

[47] *Fortunate*

city and mocked him.[48]

7. Then Elijah said, "Should I weep and fast? Is that what You want?"

8. And so it was, that he tore his clothes and put on sackcloth and fasted, and went about despondently.

9. "O LORD, I am in derision daily; everyone mocks me. You induced me, and I was persuaded. You are stronger than I, and have prevailed."

+10. Then I said, "I will not make mention of You, nor speak anymore in Your name."

11. "But Your word was in my heart and bones like a burning fire. I get weary of holding it in, and I can't do it."

12. At home he went in to his wife.

+13. But his wife accused him: "Have you been with anyone else? I heard someone say they saw you somewhere."

14. Elijah said nothing.[49]

15. Then his wife said to him, "Do you still hold to your integrity?"

16. "I have made a covenant with my eyes; why then should I gaze upon a young woman? As long as my breath is in my nostrils, my lips will not speak wickedness, nor my tongue utter deceit. My righteousness I hold fast, and will not let it go. My heart shall not reproach me as long as I live. Far be it from me that I should say you are right."

---

[48] *Elijah*
[49] *Despondently*

+17. "Until the day I die, I will not betray my integrity; it shall stand."

+18. Then a woman visited Elijah's house, and she said, "Please let the Man of God come to us again and teach us what we shall do."

19. And he said, "If the LORD does not help you, where can I find help for you? Please consider: am I God, to kill and make alive?"

+20. "Have pity on me, O you my friend, have pity on me."

+21. She came back four times with the same message, and he answered her in the same way each time.⁵⁰

22. Then she came back a fifth time: "What shall we do?"

23. So he answered, "Do not fear. Go up to your house in peace. See, I have listened to you and granted your request."

24. Then Elijah gave them just ordinances and true laws, good statutes and well-ordered commandments: a new covenant, one of life and peace. And he also had it put in writing.

25. "My words come from my upright heart. My lips utter pure knowledge: to give them light on the road which they should travel, and in the intent of the thoughts of the heart of Your people, and to fix their heart toward You."

26. And God said, "I give you every seed-bearing plant on the face of the whole earth and every tree that has fruit with seed in it. They will be yours for food. And to all the beasts of the earth and all the birds of the air and all the creatures that move on the ground, I give every

---

⁵⁰*Pity*

green plant for food."⁵¹

27. "Eat vegetables and drink water. Any kind of food can be eaten, but some foods are better than others."

28. "Honor the LORD with your possessions."

29. "A man with an evil eye hastens after riches and is unaware that poverty awaits him."

+30. "Do not withhold good from those who deserve it, when it is in the power of your hand to do so. Do not say to your neighbor, 'Go, and come back, and tomorrow I will give it,' if you could just as well give it to him or her today."

31. "Do not strive with a man without cause, if he has done you no harm."

+32. "The wicked man does deceptive work, but there is a sure reward for the sower of righteousness."

33. "An excellent wife is the crown of her husband, but she who causes shame is like rottenness in his bones."⁵²

34. "He tells the truth who states what he is sure of, but a lying witness speaks deceitfully."

+35. "The hand of the diligent will rule, but those who are lazy will be put to forced labor."

36. "He who guards his lips guards his life, but he who speaks rashly will come to ruin."

37. "The soul of a sluggard desires, and has nothing; but the soul of the diligent shall be made rich."

38. "Poverty and shame will come to him who disdains correction, but he who regards reproof will be honored."

---
⁵¹*Intent*
⁵²*Vegetables*

39. "The righteous eats to the satisfying of his soul, but the stomach of the wicked shall be in want."

40. "A truthful witness does not deceive, but a false witness pours out lies."[53]

41. "Apply your heart to instruction, and your ears to words of knowledge."

+42. "The rod of correction imparts prudence, but a child left to himself brings shame to his mother."

+43. "Don't spend all your energy on sex and all your money on women; their ways can destroy kings."

44. "It is not for kings to drink wine, nor for princes intoxicating drink; lest they forget the law and be unable to give justice to those who are oppressed."

45. "Give beer to those who are perishing, and wine to those who are bitter of heart. Let them drink and forget their poverty and remember their misery no more."

46. "Here is what I have seen: it is good and proper for a man to eat and to find satisfaction in his toilsome labor during the short life that God has given him. This is man's fate."[54]

47. "Enjoy living with the woman whom you love all the days of your fleeting and meaningless life."

48. "Those who plow iniquity and sow trouble reap the same."

49. "Every nation will be punished if it does not welcome foreigners."

---

[53] *Sluggard*
[54] *Perishing*

50. "Can you guide the stars? Can you tie the Pleiades together or loosen the belt of Orion? YAH-way made the stars, the Pleiades and Orion, and is the Lord of the whole earth."

+51. "Who are you, that you should set yourself in the place of God in human affairs? Will you never learn?"

+52. "Are you the first man who was born? Or were you made before the hills? Have you heard the counsel of God? Do you limit wisdom to yourself? What do you know that others do not know?"

53. "You cannot plumb the depths of the human heart or grasp the workings of the human mind; how then can you fathom God, who has[55] made all these things, and understand his plan?"

+54. "No, my friends, do not arouse the anger of the LORD our God."

+55. "The YAH-way will be merciful to all who do right. Let it be done diligently, for all the people and for ourselves, from the days of eternity to the ends of the earth."

+56. "You will surely be rebuked if you secretly show partiality. Take heed, do not turn to iniquity: he who does will have no quietness in his heart."

57. While he was talking, a man came near to him.

58. This man said, "My friend was in a perilous place, and he tried to commit suicide with his sword, preferring to die with honor rather than suffer humiliation at the hands of evil men."

59. "But now he is dead. Can I bring him back again? I shall go to him, but he shall not return to me."[56]

---

[55] *Meaningless*
[56] *Eternity*

+60. "What is death? The bitterness of it!"

61. "In a moment they die; in the middle of the night, people pass away."

62. "He preferred an honorable death rather than a life of disgrace."

63. "When I go the way of no return, shall we have rest together in the dust?"

64. Then Elijah replied, "Be silent and stand still, that I may reason with you. For we will surely die and become like water spilled on the ground, which cannot be gathered up again. Yet God does not take away a life."

+65. "The LORD likes to provide ways so that his banished ones can be saved."

+66. "O LORD, regard the prayer of Your servant and his supplication. May You hear us in heaven Your dwelling place, and when You hear, forgive. Forgive our temper tantrums."[57]

67. "We do not present our supplications before You because of our righteous deeds, but because of Your great mercies."

68. The LORD spoke to Elijah, "Because you have asked this thing, and have not asked long life for yourself, nor have asked riches for yourself, nor have asked the life of your enemies, behold, I have done according to your words. There has never been anyone like you. I will also give you what you didn't ask for: both riches and honor."

69. And the man said, "Let my life be valued much in the eyes of the LORD, and let Him deliver me out of all tribulation!"

---

[57] *Tantrums*

70. Then Elijah said to him, "It is good to sing praises to our God. Praise Him with the timbrel and dance, with stringed instruments and flutes; for praise is beautiful, and it is pleasant."

71. "Do not put your trust in princes, nor in a human being, in whom there is no salvation. When they die, they return to the dust; in that very day all their plans perish."[58]

+72. The man spoke to Elijah with thanksgivings. "You have shown to me much care. What can I do for you?"

73. But he said, "As the LORD lives, before whom I stand, I will receive nothing."

74. With this, he turned once more to the people.

75. Thus says the YAH-way: "The sanctuary of the LORD shall be in the center of man."

76. "Is it time for you to dwell in your paneled houses, and this temple to lie in ruins?"

77. "Now do not be rebellious, but yield yourselves to the LORD."

78. "For the LORD your God is gracious and compassionate and will not turn away from you if you return to the YAH-way."

79. "Be careful to do all that I have commanded."[59]

+80. The children of Israel brought a freewill offering to the LORD; all the men and women whose hearts were willing gave a tithe of everything that they owned.

---

[58]*Tribulation*

[59]*Compassionate*

81. "We are willing to share our possessions, including cattle and property, if you will do the same."

+82. "We have had enough to eat with plenty left over, for the LORD has blessed us with this great abundance."

83. They proclaimed a day of gladness and feasting--a holiday--for sending presents to one another and gifts to the poor. Each gave according to their ability.

84. Others sold all their remaining possessions so that the Lord would consider them worthy to be saved.

85. "May the LORD our God be with us. May he never leave us or abandon us, so that we will always live as he wants us to live, with hearts which obey his ways and commands."[60]

Five--Baruch

+1. Less than ten years passed before a cloud of gloom hung over all the people of the region.

+2. Baruch was a young man in whom there was no blemish. He was good-looking, showing intelligence in every branch of wisdom, endowed with prudence, and being able to discern knowledge.

3. He asked, "What troubles the people, that they weep?"

+4. A group of teachers said, "They don't know what truth or justice means. They make a solemn promise and then they break it!"

---

[60] *Property*

5. Then they said to one another, "We are not doing what is right. If we were, the people of Judah would be sparkling with happiness."

6. He thought about what he had heard, and tried to understand what it meant. And Baruch sat down and wept, and mourned for many days.

+7. Then Baruch became determined to renew the peace which everyone[61] longs for, and to do what was necessary to create a civilized kingdom.

8. He told his brethren: "All my life I have been honest and have tried to do what was right. I have done no wrong before you. I took good care of my fellow Jews whenever they were in need. If they were hungry, I shared my food with them; if they needed clothes, I gave them some of my own."

9. "Here I am. Witness against me before the LORD: Whose ox have I taken, or whose donkey have I taken, or whom have I defrauded? Whom have I oppressed? Have I accepted a bribe from anyone? Testify against me, and I will restore it to you."

10. And they said, "You have not defrauded us or oppressed us, nor have you taken anything from any man's hand."

11. Then Baruch said to them, "Turn around and follow me. Prepare to meet your God."

12. So Baruch stood on a platform of wood and said to all the people, "Warm[62] greetings and best wishes for your health and prosperity."

13. "Hear, O Israel, the commandments of life: listen, and know prudence."

---

[61] *Cloud*
[62] *Defrauded*

14.	"Obey the YAH-way."
15.	"Seek the LORD. You will find your God if you seek with all your heart and with all your soul."
16.	"You must obey these laws that I will tell you today, so that all will be well with you and your children, and that you may prolong your days."
+17.	"Be careful to do as the LORD your God commands; you shall not turn aside to the right hand or to the left."
+18.	The LORD says, "You should not have stood at the crossroads, nor should you have let your faith falter because of your precious children."
19.	"For those who honor Me I will honor, and those who despise Me shall[63] be lightly esteemed."
20.	"May the Lord's will be done."
21.	"He who rules over men must be just, ruling in the fear of God."
22.	"Know in your heart: as a man disciplines his son, so the LORD your God chastens you."
23.	"You shall not harden your heart or shut your hand against your poor brother, but you shall open your hand to him, and lend him sufficient for his need, whatever it may be."
24.	"Take heed lest there be a base thought in your heart, and your eye be hostile to your poor brother, and you give him nothing, and he cry to the LORD against you, and it be sin in you."
25.	"You shall give to him freely, and your heart shall not be grudging when you give to him; because for

---

[63] *Prolong*

this the LORD your God will bless you in all your work and in all that you undertake."[64]

26. "For the poor will never cease out of the land; therefore I command you, You shall open wide your hand to your brother, to the needy and to the poor, in the land."

27. "You shall appoint judges and officers in all your towns, and they shall judge the people with just judgment. You shall not pervert justice; you shall not show partiality, nor take a bribe, for a bribe blinds the eyes of the wise and twists the words of the righteous."

28. "You shall follow what is altogether just, that you may live with God."

29. "Give thanks to the God of heaven!"

30. "Let Your priests be clothed with righteousness."

31. In Jerusalem, the priests took a chest, bored a hole in its lid, and set it beside the altar, and the priests who guarded at the door put there all the money that was brought into the house of the LORD.

32. Then they gave the money, which had been apportioned, into the hands[65] of those who did the work, who had the oversight of the house of the LORD; and they paid it out to the carpenters and builders who worked on the house of the LORD, and to masons and stonecutters, and for buying timber to repair the damages in the temple.

33. So they began this good work.

+34. The people of the land tried to discourage the people of Judah, but the work proceeded with great energy and success, because the people had a mind to work.

---

[64]*Lend*
[65]*Twists*

35.	"Let it be done diligently, day by day without fail."
36.	"Is there not a time of hard service for man on the earth?"
37.	"Tremble before the God of Daniel: the living God, and enduring forever, whose kingdom is the one which shall never be destroyed."
38.	"O you who put far off the day of doom, who cause the throne of iniquity to come near. Woe to those who lie upon beds of ivory, and[66] stretch themselves upon their couches, and eat lambs from the flock, and calves from the midst of the stall; who sing idle songs to the sound of the harp, and like David invent for themselves instruments of music; who drink wine in bowls, and anoint themselves with the finest oils, but are not grieved over the ruin of Joseph!"
39.	"I will make you an object of horror because you have willingly walked by nothing but human rules and traditions learned by rote."
40.	"But if you perform My commandments, I will walk among you and be your God, and you shall be My people."
+41.	"When you sin, if you confess your iniquity, and humble your uncircumcised hearts, and accept your guilt, then there will be grace."
+42.	"I have chosen Baruch in order that he might command his household to keep the way of the LORD, to do righteousness and justice, by doing what is right in the sight of the YAH-way."
43.	Thus saith the LORD, "Cursed is the one who treats his father or his[67] mother with contempt."

---

[66] *Damages*
[67] *Horror*

44.	And all the people say, "Amen!"
45.	"Cursed is the one who has sexual intercourse with an animal."
46.	And all the people say, "Amen!"
47.	"Cursed is he who has sexual intercourse with his sister or his half-sister."
48.	And all the people say, "Amen!"
49.	"Cursed is the one who attacks his neighbor secretly."
50.	And all the people say, "Amen!"
51.	"Cursed be the deceiver."
52.	"The LORD God of Israel hates divorce, for it covers one's garment[68] with violence," says the LORD of hosts.
53.	"Now therefore, fear the LORD in sincerity and in truth. Get rid of the gods which your ancestors used to worship in Mesopotamia and in Egypt. If it seems evil to you to serve the LORD, choose for yourselves this day whom you will serve, whether the gods on the other side of the River, or the gods of the Amorites. But as for me and my house, we will serve the YAH-way."
54.	And the people replied, "Yes, we choose the LORD, for he alone is our God. We would never forsake the LORD and worship other gods!"
+55.	"If you are being truthful, God will hear you and bless you with a happy home. But if you conspire against the LORD, he will make an utter end of it."
56.	And they said, "We are among the peaceable and

---

[68]*Half-sister*

faithful. For all people walk each in the name of his god, but we will walk in the name of the LORD our God forever and ever."⁶⁹

57. Then he said, "With lies you have made the heart of the righteous sad. If the YAH-way is God, be attentive and obey. But if Baal, then follow him. How long will you falter between two opinions?"

58. The people asked, "Who?"

59. And he answered, "You."

60. The people said nothing.

+61. Then Baruch said to them, "Thus you shall say to him who lives in prosperity: Peace be to you, peace to your house, and peace to all that you have!"

62. "For the seed of peace shall be prosperous."

63. "But what peace shall there be, as long as the harlotries of your mother Jezebel and her witchcraft are so many?"

64. "Righteousness despises sinfulness, no matter how attractive it may⁷⁰ look."

65. "According to your ways and according to your deeds you shall be judged," says the Lord GOD.

66. "Woe to the shepherds of Israel who feed themselves! Should not the shepherds feed the flocks?"

+67. "Hold your tongue! Be very careful when you mention the name of the Lord."

68. "Now therefore, be pleased to look at me, for I would never lie to your face. Think it over; let there

---

⁶⁹*Mesopotamia*
⁷⁰*Baal*

be no injustice. Think it over; is there insincerity on my tongue? Cannot my taste discern falsehood?"

69. "May the Lord be with you and prosper you."

70. "Now set your heart and your soul to seek the LORD your God."

+71. "Be very careful to do the commandment and the law which Simon the[71] servant of the LORD commanded you, to love the LORD your God, to walk in all these ways, to hold tightly to YAH-way, and to serve the Holy One with all your heart and with all your soul."

72. "Be strong, and do it, that all the peoples of the earth may know that the LORD is God; there is no other."

73. "All this the LORD made me understand by His hand upon me."

Six....

1. "In the kingdom of the LORD, there the wicked cease from troubling, and there the weary are at rest. There the prisoners rest together; they do not hear the voice of the oppressor. The small and great are there, and the servant is free from his master."

2. "And they shall no longer be a prey for the nations, nor shall beasts of the land devour them; but they shall dwell safely, and no one shall[72] make them afraid."

---

[71] *Injustice*
[72] *LORD*

3. "You will remember your evil ways and your deeds that were not good, and you will change your mind and your conduct, so that there will be no more famines to disgrace you among the nations, and you will prosper in all that you do and wherever you turn."

+4. "There our daughters will be as pillars, sculptured in palace style. If the king comes to take them to be perfumers, cooks, and bakers, we will not listen or consent. But we will place them in the care of men who shall never break their heart."

5. "To whom will you liken God? Or what likeness will you compare to YAH-way?"

6. "To whom shall I be equal?" says the Holy One. "Lift up your eyes on high, and see who has created the world, and all things that come forth from it."

+7. "Who has stirred up from the East the champion of justice? Who[73] makes it happen? Who determines the course of history? I, the LORD, was there at the beginning of the generations, and I, the LORD God, will be there at the end."

8. "I form the light and create darkness, I make peace and create calamity; I, the LORD, do all these things."

9. "Woe to him who says to his father, 'What are you begetting?' or to the woman, 'What have you brought forth?'"

10. For thus says the LORD, who created the heavens, who is God, who formed the earth and made it, who has established it, who did not create it in vain, who formed it to be inhabited: "I am the LORD, and there is no other God besides Me, a just God and a Savior."

+11. "The LORD looked and was displeased that there

---

[73] Palace

was no justice, and wondered why there was no one to intervene on behalf of the truth. Therefore His own arm brought salvation: He put on righteousness as a breastplate, a helmet of protection on His head, and was clad with zeal as a cloak."[74]

12. "According to their conduct and their actions, accordingly the YAH-way will repay."

13. Thus says the LORD of hosts, the God of Israel, "Amend your ways and your doings, and I will let you dwell in this place."

14. "Be fair in your treatment of one another. If you really change your ways and your actions, and stop taking advantage of orphans, widows and foreigners, and if you do not follow other gods to your own harm, then I will let you live in this place which I gave to your fathers."

15. "And you shall know no God but Me; for there is no savior besides Me."

16. "I have heard what the prophets have said who prophesy lies in My name, saying, 'I have dreamed, I have dreamed!' How long will this be? Indeed they are prophets of the deceit of their own heart, who try to make My people forget My name by their dreams which everyone tells his neighbor."

17. "I have not sent these prophets; I have not spoken to them, yet they[75] prophesied. But if they had stood in My counsel, and had caused My people to hear My words, then they would have turned them from doing evil things."

18. "You must change the way you are living and obey the voice of the LORD your God. Now then, do it!"

---

[74] *Calamity*
[75] *Savior*

+19.   "Remember Judith. Many men wanted to marry her after the death of her husband, but she never remarried, and she lived in the house her husband had left her."

20.   "As for your adulteries and your lustful neighings, the lewdness of your prostitution on the hills in the field, I have seen your abominations. Woe to you, O Jerusalem! How long will you remain unclean?"

+21.   "When you go into the bridal chamber, and you are about to have intercourse with your bride, both of you first rise up to pray. And say, 'Blessed are you, O God of our fathers. May your name be honored forever and ever. You made Adam and you gave him his wife Eve to be[76] his help and support. You said, "It is not good for man to live alone. I will give him a suitable partner." Now, Lord, because I love her, I will not harm her. You know that I take this wife of mine not because of lust, but for a noble purpose. Please be merciful to us and allow us to live together to a happy old age. Amen, amen.'"

+22.   Thus says the LORD, "If I cause you to be carried away from Jerusalem into exile, build houses and dwell in them; plant gardens and eat their fruit. Take wives and beget sons and daughters; and take wives for your sons and give your daughters to husbands, so that they may bear sons and daughters--that you may be increased there, and not diminished. And seek the peace of the city where I have caused you to be carried away captive, and pray to Me; for in its peace you will have peace."

23.   "I will give them one heart and one way, that they may fear Me forever, for the good of them and their children after them."

24.   "They departed in tears, but I will console them and guide them. I will lead them to brooks of water, on a

---

[76]*Judith*

level road, so that none shall[77] stumble, for I am a father to Israel."

25. "Please, obey the voice of the LORD which I speak to you, so it shall be well with you, and your soul shall live."

26. "Why do you look so sad today? There is hope for your future," declares the LORD. "Ten men from every language of the nations shall grasp the sleeve of a Jewish man, saying, 'Let us go with you, for we have heard that God is with you.'"

+27. "For the LORD is the inspiration of justice."

28. "When he uttereth his voice, there is a multitude of waters in the heavens; and he causeth the vapors to ascend from the ends of the earth: he maketh lightnings with rain, and bringeth forth the wind out of his treasures."

29. "YAH-way is good to those who wait, to the soul who seeks. It is good that one should hope and wait quietly for the salvation of the LORD. It is good for a man to bear the yoke in his youth. Let him sit alone and[78] keep silent."

30. "Those who fear and love the Lord will try to please him and devote themselves to the Law."

31. "If a man has no wife, he is a sighing wanderer."

+32. "To confirm any agreement, one man should take off his sandal and give it to the other person."

33. "We should set an example for our fellow countrymen in how to be honest and faithful."

34. "O Lord, the God of our ancestors, we praise and

---

[77] *Exile*
[78] *Future*

adore you; may your name be honored forever. You have treated us as we deserve. In everything you have done to us you are always honest, and when you bring us to judgment, you are always fair."

35. The Lord says, "Jerusalem, come to the defense of widows, take the side of the fatherless, give to the poor, protect orphans, give clothing to[79] those who have none, take care of those who are broken and weak, do not make fun of those who are crippled, protect the disabled, and help the blind to catch a vision of my dazzling splendor."

+36. "As we endeavor to do this, treat us with kindness and mercy."

+37. "Honestly, no person was ever born who did not sin; there is no one living who is not guilty."

38. "So put aside all your sorrow and grief. May God Most High, the Almighty, be merciful to you and give you peace. May he give you rest from your troubles."

39. "Who then is willing on this day to give himself and all that he has to the Lord?"

+40. And Baruch knelt down on his knees and spread out his hands toward heaven, and said: "LORD God of Israel, take heed to their way."

41. "YAH-way is with you while you are with the LORD. If you seek[80] God, God will be found by you; but if you forsake the YAH-way, the LORD will forsake you."

+42. "The eyes of the Lord search back and forth across the whole earth, looking for people whose hearts are perfect, and for young men who have abstained

---

[79]*Example*
[80]*Fun*

themselves from girls and women."

+43. "A father shall not be condemned because of his children, nor shall children be accused because of their fathers, but each is to be responsible for his own sins."

44. Then all the people answered, "Amen, Amen!" while lifting up their hands; and they blessed the LORD, the great God.

45. Then he said to them, "Go your way, eat the fat, drink the sweet, and send portions to those in need."

46. So they sang praises with gladness, accompanied by loud instruments, because they understood the words that were declared to them.[81]

47. They ate and were filled and grew fat, and delighted themselves in Your great goodness; everyone whose spirit God had stirred.

+48. There was a time when Baruch had thought that the LORD had treated him cruelly. However God turned the curse into a blessing. Indeed the LORD gave Baruch twice as much as he had before, for this was right in the eyes of all the people.[82]

---

[81] *Instruments*
[82] *Fat*

Works Cited

History

35000	www.lulu.com/shop/mike-marty/35000/ebook/product-23576749.html (Retrieved 4/11/25)
administer	www.lulu.com/shop/mike-marty/administer/ebook/product-23576836.html (Retrieved 4/11/25)
ambassadors	www.lulu.com/shop/mike-marty/ambassadors/ebook/product-23576795.html (Retrieved 4/11/25)
ancient	www.lulu.com/shop/mike-marty/ancient/ebook/product-23576780.html (Retrieved 4/11/25)
baby	https://www.barnesandnoble.com/w/baby-mike-marty/1128288516 (Retrieved 4/12/25)
Bel	https://www.barnesandnoble.com/w/bel-mike-marty/1128283577 (Retrieved 4/12/25)
beware	https://www.barnesandnoble.com/w/beware-mike-marty/1128261051 (Retrieved 4/12/25)
capture	https://www.barnesandnoble.com/w/capture-mike-marty/1128229134 (Retrieved 4/12/25)
circumcise	https://www.barnesandnoble.com/w/circumcise-mike-marty/1128223564 (Retrieved 4/12/25)
confused	www.barnesandnoble.com/w/confused-mike-spiritfair-marty/1126977292 (Retrieved 4/12/25)
contention	www.barnesandnoble.com/w/contention-mike-spiritfair-marty/1126963863 (Retrieved 4/12/25)
Daniel	https://www.barnesandnoble.com/w/daniel-mike-marty/1128171108 (Retrieved 4/12/25)
dismayed	www.barnesandnoble.com/w/dismayed-mike-spiritfair-marty/1126972574 (Retrieved 4/12/25)
dumbfounded	www.barnesandnoble.com/w/dumbfounded-mike-spiritfair-marty/1126958203 (Retrieved 4/12/25)
dungeon	www.barnesandnoble.com/w/dungeon-mike-spiritfair-marty/1126958262 (Retrieved 4/12/25)
encouraged	https://www.barnesandnoble.com/w/encouraged-mike-marty/1128115680 (Retrieved 4/12/25)
equity	https://www.barnesandnoble.com/w/equity-mike-marty/1128103830 (Retrieved 4/12/25)
escape	www.barnesandnoble.com/w/escape-mike-spiritfair-marty/1126982570 (Retrieved 4/12/25)
establish	https://www.barnesandnoble.com/w/establish-mike-marty/1128088460 (Retrieved 4/12/25)
exquisite	www.barnesandnoble.com/w/exquisite-mike-spiritfair-marty/1126958280 (Retrieved 4/12/25)
greedy	https://www.barnesandnoble.com/w/greedy-mike-marty/1128058829 (Retrieved 4/12/25)
half	https://www.barnesandnoble.com/w/half-mike-marty/1128029779 (Retrieved 4/12/25)
Hebrew	https://www.barnesandnoble.com/w/hebrew-mike-marty/1128018578 (Retrieved 4/12/25)
hideout	https://www.barnesandnoble.com/w/hideout-mike-marty/1128015762 (Retrieved 4/12/25)
holy	www.lulu.com/shop/mike-marty/holy/ebook/product-23699052.html (Retrieved 4/12/25)
huddled	www.barnesandnoble.com/w/huddled-mike-spiritfair-marty/1126977339 (Retrieved 4/12/25)
idols	https://www.barnesandnoble.com/w/idols-mike-marty/1127976671 (Retrieved 4/12/25)
instruct	https://www.barnesandnoble.com/w/instruct-mike-marty/1127968643 (Retrieved 4/12/25)
intuition	www.barnesandnoble.com/w/intuition-mike-spiritfair-marty/1126972488 (Retrieved 4/12/25)
Jerusalem	https://www.barnesandnoble.com/w/jerusalem-mike-marty/1127948851 (Retrieved 4/12/25)
judge	https://www.kobo.com/us/en/ebook/judge-12 (Retrieved 4/12/25)
Mattathias	https://www.barnesandnoble.com/w/mattathias-mike-marty/1127942524 (Retrieved 4/12/25)
Ninevah	https://www.barnesandnoble.com/w/ninevah-mike-marty/1127936868 (Retrieved 4/12/25)
nonexistent	https://www.barnesandnoble.com/w/nonexistent-mike-marty/1127925970 (Retrieved 4/12/25)
penitence	https://www.barnesandnoble.com/w/penitence-mike-marty/1127916033 (Retrieved 4/12/25)
pursued	www.barnesandnoble.com/w/pursued-mike-spiritfair-marty/1126958266 (Retrieved 4/12/25)
responsive	www.barnesandnoble.com/w/responsive-mike-spiritfair-marty/1126972341 (Retrieved 4/12/25)
righteousness	www.barnesandnoble.com/w/righteousness-mike-spiritfair-marty/1126977309 (Retrieved 4/12/25)
sackcloth	https://www.barnesandnoble.com/w/sackcloth-mike-marty/1127866131 (Retrieved 4/12/25)
Saul	https://www.barnesandnoble.com/w/saul-mike-marty/1127848403 (Retrieved 4/12/25)
shamefully	www.barnesandnoble.com/w/shamefully-mike-spiritfair-marty/1126977286 (Retrieved 4/12/25)
spirits	www.lulu.com/shop/mike-marty/spirits/ebook/product-23728488.html (Retrieved 4/12/25)
strife	www.barnesandnoble.com/w/strife-mike-spiritfair-marty/1126941186 (Retrieved 4/12/25)

strong	www.barnesandnoble.com/w/strong-mike-spiritfair-marty/1126941176 (Retrieved 4/12/25)
success	www.barnesandnoble.com/w/success-mike-spiritfair-marty/1126941208 (Retrieved 4/12/25)
table	https://www.barnesandnoble.com/w/table-mike-marty/1127499835 (Retrieved 4/12/25)
threatened	https://www.barnesandnoble.com/w/threatened-mike-marty/1127626579 (Retrieved 4/12/25)
Truth	www.barnesandnoble.com/w/truth-mike-spiritfair-marty/1126963744 (Retrieved 4/12/25)
whispered	https://www.barnesandnoble.com/w/whispered-mike-marty/1127585651 (Retrieved 4/12/25)
word	https://www.barnesandnoble.com/w/word-mike-marty/1001011540 (Retrieved 4/12/25)
YAH-way	https://www.barnesandnoble.com/w/yah-way-mike-marty/1127548252 (Retrieved 4/12/25)
yearned	https://www.barnesandnoble.com/w/yearned-mike-marty/1127538834 (Retrieved 4/12/25)
Zion	https://www.barnesandnoble.com/w/zion-mike-marty/1127525195 (Retrieved 4/12/25)

Poetry

Abishag	www.lulu.com/shop/mike-marty/abishag/ebook/product-23766996.html (Retrieved 4/13/25)
barley	www.lulu.com/shop/mike-marty/barley/ebook/product-23780099.html (Retrieved 4/13/25)
bathe	www.lulu.com/shop/mike-marty/bathe/ebook/product-23780103.html (Retrieved 4/13/25)
bethink	www.lulu.com/shop/mike-marty/bethink/ebook/product-23780109.html (Retrieved 4/13/25)
bitch	www.lulu.com/shop/mike-marty/bitch/ebook/product-23781754.html (Retrieved 4/13/25)
Boaz	www.lulu.com/shop/mike-marty/boaz/ebook/product-23781795.html (Retrieved 4/13/25)
bodies	www.lulu.com/shop/mike-marty/bodies/ebook/product-23781808.html (Retrieved 4/13/25)
breasts	https://www.kobo.com/us/en/ebook/breasts-3 (Retrieved 4/13/25)
Cherokee	https://www.kobo.com/us/en/ebook/cherokee-16 (Retrieved 4/13/25)
clamorous	www.lulu.com/shop/mike-marty/clamorous/ebook/product-23784629.html (Retrieved 4/13/25)
	https://youtu.be/PZMhRF8cTPg
closed	www.lulu.com/shop/mike-marty/closed/ebook/product-23784642.html (Retrieved 4/13/25)
confessing	www.lulu.com/shop/mike-marty/confessing/ebook/product-23786386.html (Retrieved 4/13/25)
deeply	www.lulu.com/shop/mike-marty/deeply/ebook/product-23787977.html (Retrieved 4/13/25)
delight	www.lulu.com/shop/mike-marty/delight/ebook/product-23788003.html (Retrieved 4/13/25)
distinguished	https://www.kobo.com/us/en/ebook/distinguished-1 (Retrieved 4/13/25)
Esther	www.lulu.com/shop/mike-marty/esther/ebook/product-23793527.html (Retrieved 4/13/25)
everlasting	www.lulu.com/shop/mike-marty/everlasting/ebook/product-23793566.html (Retrieved 4/13/25)
filthy	www.lulu.com/shop/mike-marty/filthy/ebook/product-23798767.html (Retrieved 4/13/25)
fists	www.lulu.com/shop/mike-marty/fists/ebook/product-23798797.html (Retrieved 4/13/25)
forgive	www.lulu.com/shop/mike-marty/forgive/ebook/product-23798814.html (Retrieved 4/13/25)
generations	www.lulu.com/shop/mike-marty/generations/ebook/product-23802109.html (Retrieved 4/13/25)
hidden	www.lulu.com/shop/mike-marty/hidden/ebook/product-23804838.html (Retrieved 4/13/25)
honeybuns	https://www.kobo.com/us/en/ebook/honeybuns-1 (Retrieved 4/13/25)
honorable	www.lulu.com/shop/mike-marty/honorable/ebook/product-23804861.html (Retrieved 4/13/25)
ignorant	www.lulu.com/shop/mike-marty/ignorant/ebook/product-23805999.html (Retrieved 4/13/25)
innocent	www.lulu.com/shop/mike-marty/innocent/ebook/product-23808977.html (Retrieved 4/13/25)
ivory	https://www.kobo.com/us/en/ebook/ivory-14 (Retrieved 4/13/25)
Joebh	www.lulu.com/shop/mike-marty/joebh/ebook/product-23810648.html (Retrieved 4/13/25)
kindle	www.lulu.com/shop/mike-marty/kindle/ebook/product-23812279.html (Retrieved 4/13/25)
liberality	www.lulu.com/shop/mike-marty/liberality/ebook/product-23814662.html (Retrieved 4/13/25)
lovers	www.lulu.com/shop/mike-marty/lovers/ebook/product-23814668.html (Retrieved 4/13/25)
nurse	www.lulu.com/shop/mike-marty/nurse/ebook/product-23819014.html (Retrieved 4/13/25)
pause	www.lulu.com/shop/mike-marty/pause/ebook/product-23519853.html (Retrieved 4/13/25)
pedestal	https://www.kobo.com/us/en/ebook/pedestal-1 (Retrieved 4/13/25)
petition	https://www.kobo.com/us/en/ebook/petition-1 (Retrieved 4/13/25)
plentiful	https://www.kobo.com/us/en/ebook/plentiful-1 (Retrieved 4/13/25)
ravished	https://www.kobo.com/us/en/ebook/ravished-13 (Retrieved 4/13/25)
robbed	https://www.kobo.com/us/en/ebook/robbed-2 (Retrieved 4/13/25)
Ruth	https://www.kobo.com/us/en/ebook/ruth-74 (Retrieved 4/13/25)
Sarah	https://www.kobo.com/us/en/ebook/sarah-55 (Retrieved 4/13/25)
satisfy	https://www.kobo.com/us/en/ebook/satisfy (Retrieved 4/13/25)
scepter	https://www.kobo.com/us/en/ebook/scepter-1 (Retrieved 4/13/25)
skipping	https://www.kobo.com/us/en/ebook/skipping-1 (Retrieved 4/13/25)
smitten	https://www.kobo.com/us/en/ebook/smitten-24 (Retrieved 4/13/25)
stallion	https://www.kobo.com/us/en/ebook/stallion-3 (Retrieved 4/13/25)
surprised	https://www.kobo.com/us/en/ebook/surprised-2 (Retrieved 4/13/25)
Susanna	https://www.kobo.com/us/en/ebook/susanna-7 (Retrieved 4/13/25)

thighs	https://www.kobo.com/us/en/ebook/thighs (Retrieved 4/13/25)
throat	https://www.kobo.com/us/en/ebook/throat-2 (Retrieved 4/13/25)
Tobit	https://www.kobo.com/us/en/ebook/tobit-3 (Retrieved 4/13/25)
unpretentious	https://www.kobo.com/us/en/ebook/unpretentious (Retrieved 4/13/25)
Uz	https://www.kobo.com/us/en/ebook/uz (Retrieved 4/13/25)
Vashti	https://www.kobo.com/us/en/ebook/vashti-1 (Retrieved 4/13/25)
waywardness	https://www.kobo.com/us/en/ebook/waywardness (Retrieved 4/13/25)
wonderful	https://www.kobo.com/us/en/ebook/wonderful-11 (Retrieved 4/13/25)
wounded	https://www.kobo.com/us/en/ebook/wounded-23 (Retrieved 4/13/25)
Xerxes	https://www.kobo.com/us/en/ebook/xerxes-11 (Retrieved 4/13/25)

Piety

accusation	www.lulu.com/shop/mike-marty/accusation/ebook/product-23768461.html (Retrieved 4/13/25)
animal	www.lulu.com/shop/mike-marty/animal/ebook/product-23773913.html (Retrieved 4/13/25)
aunt	www.lulu.com/shop/mike-marty/aunt/ebook/product-23777625.html (Retrieved 4/13/25)
Baal	www.lulu.com/shop/mike-marty/baal/ebook/product-23780091.html (Retrieved 4/13/25)
calamity	www.lulu.com/shop/mike-marty/calamity/ebook/product-23781822.html (Retrieved 4/13/25)
cloud	www.lulu.com/shop/mike-marty/cloud/ebook/product-23784655.html (Retrieved 4/13/25)
compassionate	www.lulu.com/shop/mike-marty/compassionate/ebook/product-23784662.html (Retrieved 4/13/25)
confounded	www.lulu.com/shop/mike-marty/confounded/ebook/product-23786399.html (Retrieved 4/13/25)
congregation	www.lulu.com/shop/mike-marty/congregation/ebook/product-23786412.html (Retrieved 4/13/25)
courteous	www.lulu.com/shop/mike-marty/courteous/ebook/product-23786427.html (Retrieved 4/13/25)
damages	www.lulu.com/shop/mike-marty/damages/ebook/product-23787960.html (Retrieved 4/13/25)
defrauded	www.lulu.com/shop/mike-marty/defrauded/ebook/product-23787991.html (Retrieved 4/13/25)
despondently	www.lulu.com/shop/mike-marty/despondently/ebook/product-23790247.html (Retrieved 4/13/25) https://youtu.be/fXhIHgo6e-4
diseases	www.lulu.com/shop/mike-marty/diseases/ebook/product-23790261.html (Retrieved 4/13/25)
dislike	www.lulu.com/shop/mike-marty/dislike/ebook/product-23790272.html (Retrieved 4/13/25)
drunk	www.lulu.com/shop/mike-marty/drunk/ebook/product-23790291.html (Retrieved 4/13/25)
Elijah	www.lulu.com/shop/mike-marty/elijah/ebook/product-23792855.html (Retrieved 4/13/25)
entices	www.lulu.com/shop/mike-marty/entices/ebook/product-23792858.html (Retrieved 4/13/25)
estate	www.lulu.com/shop/mike-marty/estate/ebook/product-23792865.html (Retrieved 4/13/25)
eternity	www.lulu.com/shop/mike-marty/eternity/ebook/product-23793537.html (Retrieved 4/13/25)
example	www.lulu.com/shop/mike-marty/example/ebook/product-23793583.html (Retrieved 4/13/25)
exile	www.lulu.com/shop/mike-marty/exile/ebook/product-23796130.html (Retrieved 4/13/25)
explode	www.lulu.com/shop/mike-marty/explode/ebook/product-23796140.html (Retrieved 4/13/25)
expression	www.lulu.com/shop/mike-marty/expression/ebook/product-23796152.html (Retrieved 4/13/25)
fat	www.lulu.com/shop/mike-marty/fat/ebook/product-23796169.html (Retrieved 4/13/25)
foliage	www.lulu.com/shop/mike-marty/foliage/ebook/product-23798805.html (Retrieved 4/13/25)
fortunate	www.lulu.com/shop/mike-marty/fortunate/ebook/product-23800423.html (Retrieved 4/13/25)
fraud	www.lulu.com/shop/mike-marty/fraud/ebook/product-23800431.html (Retrieved 4/13/25)
fun	www.lulu.com/shop/mike-marty/fun/ebook/product-23800439.html (Retrieved 4/13/25)
future	www.lulu.com/shop/mike-marty/future/ebook/product-23800447.html (Retrieved 4/13/25)
gluttony	www.lulu.com/shop/mike-marty/gluttony/ebook/product-23802120.html (Retrieved 4/13/25)
groans	www.lulu.com/shop/mike-marty/groans/ebook/product-23802133.html (Retrieved 4/13/25)
half-sister	www.lulu.com/shop/mike-marty/half-sister/ebook/product-23802146.html (Retrieved 4/13/25)
hearing	www.lulu.com/shop/mike-marty/hearing/ebook/product-23804822.html (Retrieved 4/13/25)
horror	www.lulu.com/shop/mike-marty/horror/ebook/product-23805985.html (Retrieved 4/13/25)
impose	www.lulu.com/shop/mike-marty/impose/ebook/product-23806009.html (Retrieved 4/13/25)
influence	www.lulu.com/shop/mike-marty/influence/ebook/product-23806016.html (Retrieved 4/13/25)
injustice	www.lulu.com/shop/mike-marty/injustice/ebook/product-23808965.html (Retrieved 4/13/25)
instruments	www.lulu.com/shop/mike-marty/instruments/ebook/product-23808992.html (Retrieved 4/13/25)
Intelligence	www.lulu.com/shop/mike-marty/intelligence/ebook/product-23808997.html (Retrieved 4/13/25)
intent	www.lulu.com/shop/mike-marty/intent/ebook/product-23810641.html (Retrieved 4/13/25)
jubilee	www.lulu.com/shop/mike-marty/jubilee/ebook/product-23810663.html (Retrieved 4/13/25)
Judith	www.lulu.com/shop/mike-marty/judith/ebook/product-23810670.html (Retrieved 4/13/25)
know	www.lulu.com/shop/mike-marty/know/ebook/product-23812298.html (Retrieved 4/13/25)
labor	www.lulu.com/shop/mike-marty/labor/ebook/product-23812324.html (Retrieved 4/13/25)
lend	www.lulu.com/shop/mike-marty/lend/ebook/product-23812352.html (Retrieved 4/13/25)
lewdness	www.lulu.com/shop/mike-marty/lewdness/ebook/product-23814646.html (Retrieved 4/13/25)

LORD	https://www.amazon.com/dp/B0758GNG2Q (Retrieved 4/13/25)
mansions	www.lulu.com/shop/mike-marty/mansions/ebook/product-23814681.html (Retrieved 4/13/25)
meaningless	www.lulu.com/shop/mike-marty/meaningless/ebook/product-23817621.html (Retrieved 4/13/25)
Mesopotamia	www.lulu.com/shop/mike-marty/mesopotamia/ebook/product-23817633.html (Retrieved 4/13/25)
	https://youtu.be/StrRF5hiGAc
mindful	www.lulu.com/shop/mike-marty/mindful/ebook/product-23817667.html (Retrieved 4/13/25)
nourishment	https://www.amazon.com/dp/B076KSZZ73 (Retrieved 4/13/25)
palace	www.lulu.com/shop/mike-marty/palace/ebook/product-23819020.html (Retrieved 4/13/25)
perishing	www.lulu.com/shop/mike-marty/perishing/ebook/product-23819030.html (Retrieved 4/13/25)
pity	www.lulu.com/shop/mike-marty/pity/ebook/product-23820963.html (Retrieved 4/13/25)
prolong	www.lulu.com/shop/mike-marty/prolong/ebook/product-23820976.html (Retrieved 4/13/25)
property	www.lulu.com/shop/mike-marty/property/ebook/product-23821009.html (Retrieved 4/13/25)
purpose	www.lulu.com/shop/mike-marty/purpose/ebook/product-23823264.html (Retrieved 4/13/25)
quantity	www.lulu.com/shop/mike-marty/quantity/ebook/product-23823268.html (Retrieved 4/13/25)
quenched	www.lulu.com/shop/mike-marty/quenched/ebook/product-23823283.html (Retrieved 4/13/25)
quiver	https://www.barnesandnoble.com/w/quiver-mike-marty/1127948094 (Retrieved 4/13/25)
rebuke	https://www.kobo.com/us/en/ebook/rebuke-2 (Retrieved 4/13/25)
reputation	https://www.kobo.com/us/en/ebook/reputation-9 (Retrieved 4/13/25)
revelations	https://www.kobo.com/us/en/ebook/revelations-128 (Retrieved 4/13/25)
Satan	www.lulu.com/shop/mike-marty/satan/ebook/product-23506076.html (Retrieved 4/13/25)
savior	https://www.kobo.com/us/en/ebook/savior-29 (Retrieved 4/13/25)
semen	https://www.kobo.com/us/en/ebook/semen-2 (Retrieved 4/13/25)
Simon	https://www.kobo.com/us/en/ebook/simon-39 (Retrieved 4/13/25)
sluggard	https://www.kobo.com/us/en/ebook/sluggard-1 (Retrieved 4/13/25)
	https://youtu.be/GiB57pGH8Xk
slurp	https://www.kobo.com/us/en/ebook/slurp-4 (Retrieved 4/13/25)
sojourner	https://www.kobo.com/us/en/ebook/sojourner-10 (Retrieved 4/13/25)
storm	https://www.kobo.com/us/en/ebook/storm-82 (Retrieved 4/13/25)
	https://youtu.be/lhx3k8AjFCk
suspicious	https://www.kobo.com/us/en/ebook/suspicious-11 (Retrieved 4/13/25)
tantrums	https://www.kobo.com/us/en/ebook/tantrums-4 (Retrieved 4/13/25)
tolerate	https://www.kobo.com/us/en/ebook/tolerate-1 (Retrieved 4/13/25)
transgression	https://www.amazon.com/dp/B0773Q6KLH (Retrieved 4/13/25)
traveler	https://www.kobo.com/us/en/ebook/traveler-17 (Retrieved 4/13/25)
	https://youtu.be/oAN3Owo_VMo
tribulation	https://www.kobo.com/us/en/ebook/tribulation-16 (Retrieved 4/13/25)
twists	https://www.kobo.com/us/en/ebook/twists-1 (Retrieved 4/13/25)
	https://youtu.be/zW_6Jfldf1s
vegetables	https://www.kobo.com/us/en/ebook/vegetables-10 (Retrieved 4/13/25)
welcome	https://www.kobo.com/us/en/ebook/welcome-15 (Retrieved 4/13/25)

www.ingramcontent.com/pod-product-compliance
Lightning Source LLC
Chambersburg PA
CBHW052032030426

42337CB00027B/4965